RESTORATIVE JUSTICE FOR SEXUAL ABUSE
Healing Wounds

DR. MAXWELL SHIMBA

Shimba Publishing LLC
Printed in the United States of America

First Printing Edition, 2023

TABLE OF CONTENTS

INTRODUCTION

Sexual abuse is a deeply troubling and pervasive issue that casts a long, dark shadow over individuals and communities worldwide. At its core, it represents a grave violation of human dignity, autonomy, and consent. From the unrelenting pain it inflicts on survivors to the insidious ripple effects felt by families, friends, and entire societies, sexual abuse is a problem that transcends boundaries of geography, age, gender, race, and socioeconomic status. It is a universal crisis that demands our unwavering attention and a holistic, compassionate response.

The scars left by sexual abuse are not merely physical but run deep into the emotional and psychological fabric of survivors. These wounds are often hidden, yet they shape the course of lives, challenging the very foundations of trust, safety, and justice within society. Survivors of sexual abuse grapple with a complex tapestry of emotions, including fear, shame, guilt, and a profound sense of violation. These emotions can fester over time, leaving individuals struggling to rebuild their shattered sense of self and navigate a world that often fails to understand their trauma.

In the wake of sexual abuse, not only is the survivor's well-being at stake, but the broader societal framework is also put to the test. Communities are left grappling with questions of responsibility, support, and justice. The traditional criminal justice systems, designed for retribution, often fall short in addressing the nuanced dynamics of sexual abuse cases. Inadequate support, punitive measures, and a lack of empathy can leave survivors feeling retraumatized and unheard. This stark reality underscores the urgent need for a restorative approach—a path toward healing, accountability, and reconciliation.

This book embarks on an introductory exploration of the multifaceted topic of sexual abuse, recognizing the urgent demand for a restorative approach to bring about meaningful change. In the pages that follow, we will delve deeper into the principles of restorative justice and their application in sexual abuse cases. We will explore the trauma experienced by survivors and the intricacies of restorative dialogues, all while providing practical insights into the process. Our objective is to shed light on how a restorative approach can contribute to the healing of survivors and the transformation of communities impacted by sexual abuse, ultimately fostering a safer and more compassionate world for all.

CHAPTER 1

UNDERSTANDING THE PROBLEM OF SEXUAL ABUSE

Understanding the problem of sexual abuse is of paramount importance for several reasons:

What is Sexual Abuse?

Sexual abuse is a term encompassing a wide range of actions that involve non-consensual sexual contact or exploitation. It includes but is not limited to acts such as harassment, assault, molestation, and rape. Sexual abuse occurs when an individual's autonomy and consent are violated, leading to physical, emotional, and psychological harm.

Violation of Autonomy and Consent:

Sexual abuse is a profound violation of an individual's autonomy and consent. Autonomy refers to a person's right to make decisions about their own body and sexuality. Consent, in this context, means freely and willingly agreeing to any sexual activity. Sexual abuse involves disregarding these fundamental rights, imposing sexual acts on someone against their will, and depriving them of their agency and dignity.

No Boundaries of Age, Gender, Race, or Socioeconomic Status:

Sexual abuse knows no boundaries. It transcends age, gender, race, and socioeconomic status. It can affect anyone, regardless of their background or circumstances. Victims and survivors of sexual abuse come from all walks of life, emphasizing that this issue is not isolated to specific groups or demographics. This universality underscores the importance of addressing sexual abuse as a societal problem that demands attention and action from everyone.

Consequences Ripple Through Society:

The consequences of sexual abuse extend far beyond the immediate victim. They reverberate through society in various ways. Families, friends, and communities are impacted as they provide support to survivors. Trust in interpersonal relationships and institutions can erode. The trauma and aftermath of sexual abuse affect workplaces, schools, and neighborhoods. It is a pervasive issue that affects the social fabric and well-being of society as a whole.

Importance of Learning the Sobering Realities:

Learning about the sobering realities of sexual abuse is essential for several reasons. First, it raises awareness about the prevalence of the issue, dispelling any misconceptions and denial. Second, it emphasizes the urgent need for support systems, prevention, and intervention strategies. Third, it acknowledges the profound and lasting trauma experienced by survivors, emphasizing the importance of empathy and appropriate responses. Ultimately, understanding the problem of sexual abuse is the first step in addressing it effectively, promoting justice, and fostering a society where consent, respect, and safety are upheld as fundamental principles.

The need for a restorative approach in cases of sexual abuse is of paramount importance for several compelling reasons:

Inadequacies of Traditional Criminal Justice Systems:

Traditional criminal justice systems are designed with a primary focus on punitive measures and adversarial proceedings. While they serve an essential role in society, they often struggle to address the intricate dynamics of sexual abuse cases. The courtroom environment can be intimidating and retraumatizing for survivors, who may feel overwhelmed and silenced. Moreover, the emphasis on proving guilt and assigning punishment can inadvertently overshadow the needs of survivors for healing and closure.

Unmet Support and Healing Needs:

Survivors of sexual abuse have unique emotional and psychological needs that go beyond punitive justice. They often require support, empathy, and opportunities for healing to rebuild their lives. Traditional justice systems, by prioritizing punishment, may not adequately address these critical aspects of recovery, leaving survivors feeling unsupported and unheard.

The Restorative Approach:

A restorative approach to sexual abuse cases recognizes that justice should extend beyond punishment and retribution. It places healing, empathy, accountability, and the restoration of shattered lives at its core. Restorative justice principles encourage open and respectful communication, allowing survivors to voice their experiences, confront their offenders, and find closure in a safe and supportive environment. This approach aims to address the harm done, promote accountability and empathy, and facilitate the survivor's journey toward recovery.

Alternative Path to Justice and Recovery:

Restorative justice principles provide an alternative path to justice and recovery in sexual abuse cases. By engaging survivors, offenders, and communities in a dialogue-based process, it encourages them to actively participate in resolving the harm caused. This approach can lead to a deeper understanding of the consequences of sexual abuse, promote accountability, and offer survivors a chance to be heard and validated. Ultimately, it seeks to restore the balance of power and dignity to survivors and foster a sense of closure and healing.

In summary, the pressing need for a restorative approach in sexual abuse cases arises from the shortcomings of traditional criminal justice systems and the unique needs of survivors. By emphasizing healing, empathy, accountability, and restoration, restorative justice principles offer an alternative and more holistic path to justice and recovery that recognizes the profound impact of sexual abuse and seeks to address it in a more comprehensive and compassionate manner.

CHAPTER 2

DEFINING RESTORATIVE JUSTICE

Restorative Justice:

Restorative justice is a transformative approach to resolving conflicts and addressing harm that focuses on healing, accountability, and reconciliation rather than punishment. It seeks to repair the harm caused by an offense by involving all parties affected—victims, offenders, and communities—in a collaborative process aimed at understanding the impact, taking responsibility, and finding ways to make amends. This approach prioritizes the restoration of relationships, the empowerment of survivors, and the reintegration of offenders into the community.

Core Principles of Restorative Justice:

1. Accountability: Restorative justice emphasizes that individuals who cause harm should take responsibility for their actions. This accountability involves acknowledging the harm done, understanding its consequences, and actively participating in making amends.

2. Empathy: Empathy is a central principle of restorative justice, encouraging all parties involved to listen and understand each other's perspectives and feelings. This empathetic understanding fosters compassion and helps in the healing process.

3. Inclusivity: Restorative justice strives to involve all stakeholders affected by an offense, including the victim, the offender, and the community. Inclusivity ensures that everyone's needs and concerns are considered in the resolution process.

4. Repairing Harm: The primary goal of restorative justice is to repair the harm caused by an offense. This involves addressing the tangible and intangible consequences of the wrongdoing and finding ways to restore a sense of balance and justice.

5. Voluntary Participation: Participation in the restorative justice process is voluntary, allowing individuals to engage willingly. This ensures that the process is based on consent and respect for all parties involved.

6. Collaborative Decision-Making: Restorative justice promotes collaborative decision-making, where all stakeholders actively contribute to developing and implementing solutions. This collaborative approach increases the likelihood of mutually agreed-upon outcomes.

7. Community Involvement: Communities play a crucial role in the restorative justice process. They provide support and guidance, hold individuals accountable, and contribute to the reintegration of offenders into society.

8. Long-Term Healing: Restorative justice recognizes that healing and recovery are ongoing processes. It aims to provide lasting solutions that address the needs of survivors and support the rehabilitation of offenders.

9. Conflict Transformation: Instead of perpetuating cycles of harm and retaliation, restorative justice seeks to

transform conflicts into opportunities for growth, understanding, and positive change.

These core principles serve as the foundation of restorative justice and guide the restorative process. In cases of sexual abuse, these principles play a vital role in facilitating healing, accountability, and reconciliation, as they provide a framework for addressing the profound harm caused by such offenses in a holistic and empathetic manner.

Historical Context and Evolution of Restorative Justice:

To comprehend the essence of restorative justice, it is crucial to examine its historical context and evolutionary journey, tracing its roots from indigenous and traditional origins to its contemporary application. This historical exploration provides invaluable insights into the foundations and development of this transformative approach.

Roots in Indigenous and Traditional Practices:

Restorative justice has ancient roots, often found in the practices of indigenous and traditional societies. Many indigenous cultures around the world have long embraced principles of healing, reconciliation, and community involvement in resolving conflicts and addressing harm. These practices prioritize restoration, accountability, and the restoration of relationships over punitive measures.

Historical Influences:

Restorative justice was influenced by various historical movements and philosophies. In Europe, for example, the idea of restitution and compensation was present in medieval law systems. Similarly, concepts of penance and reconciliation within religious traditions contributed to the development of restorative principles.

Modern Revival and Formalization:

The modern revival of restorative justice can be traced to the mid-20th century, particularly in the fields of criminology and sociology. Scholars and practitioners began to recognize the limitations of punitive justice systems and sought alternative approaches. Early pioneers, such as Howard Zehr and Mark Umbreit, played pivotal roles in formalizing restorative justice practices.

Adaptation to Changing Societal Needs:

Restorative justice has evolved over time to address the changing needs and complexities of society. It has expanded beyond its initial focus on criminal justice to encompass a broader range of conflicts, including family disputes, school discipline, and workplace issues. This adaptability highlights its versatility and applicability in various contexts.

Understanding the Historical Context:

Understanding the historical context of restorative justice is essential for several reasons. First, it allows us to appreciate the rich tapestry of influences that have shaped this approach, acknowledging its global and multidisciplinary roots. Second, it offers a historical precedent for the principles and practices of restorative justice, demonstrating that these ideas have deep historical resonance.

Moreover, recognizing the evolution of restorative justice helps us understand its capacity to adapt to the complexities of contemporary society. It highlights the ongoing development of restorative principles and practices, ensuring that they remain relevant and effective in addressing modern challenges, including the sensitive and intricate issues surrounding sexual abuse.

Restorative vs. Retributive Justice:

Retributive Justice:

Retributive justice is the more traditional and punitive approach to addressing wrongdoing. Its primary focus is on punishing offenders as a means of retribution and deterrence. Key characteristics of retributive justice include:

1. Punishment-Centered: Retributive justice centers on punishing offenders for their actions. The severity of the punishment is often determined by the seriousness of the offense and the legal system's guidelines.

2. Adversarial Process: The legal system in retributive justice is adversarial, with a clear distinction between the prosecution and defense. The process is designed to prove guilt and assign punishment.

3. Lack of Victim Involvement: While victims play a role in retributive justice as witnesses, they often have limited involvement in decision-making or restitution processes. The focus is primarily on the state vs. the offender.

4. Goal of Deterrence: Retributive justice aims to deter future wrongdoing by making the punishment severe enough to discourage potential offenders. The idea is that the fear of punishment will prevent crimes.

Restorative Justice:

Restorative justice, on the other hand, takes a fundamentally different approach to addressing harm and wrongdoing. It prioritizes healing, reconciliation, and the repair of harm over punishment. Key characteristics of restorative justice include:

1. Healing-Centered: Restorative justice seeks to heal the harm caused by an offense. It places a strong emphasis on the needs of victims, survivors, and the community affected.

2. Collaborative Process: Restorative justice promotes a collaborative process that involves victims, offenders, and the community. The focus is on open communication, understanding, and addressing the root causes of harm.

3. Empathy and Accountability: Restorative justice encourages empathy and accountability. Offenders are encouraged to take responsibility for their actions, understand the impact on victims, and make amends.

4. Restitution and Reconciliation: The goal of restorative justice is to make restitution to the victim and achieve reconciliation between the parties involved. This can involve apologies, community service, or other measures agreed upon by all stakeholders.

Why Restorative Justice for Sexual Abuse:
Restorative justice is uniquely suited to address the sensitive and intricate issues surrounding sexual abuse for several reasons:

1. Empowerment of Survivors: Restorative justice empowers survivors by giving them a voice in the process. It allows them to express their feelings, ask questions, and seek answers, which can be especially important in cases of sexual abuse.

2. Accountability with Healing: It holds offenders accountable for their actions while focusing on their rehabilitation and reintegration into the community. This approach acknowledges that sexual offenders can also benefit from a path toward healing and transformation.

3. Trauma-Informed: Restorative justice is trauma-informed, recognizing the profound trauma experienced by survivors of sexual abuse. It aims to minimize retraumatization by providing a safe and supportive environment.

4. Community Support: Restorative justice involves the community, which can provide essential support to survivors and contribute to offender accountability and reintegration.

In summary, the fundamental differences between restorative and retributive justice lie in their approaches to addressing harm and wrongdoing. While retributive justice focuses on punishment and deterrence, restorative justice prioritizes healing, reconciliation, and the repair of harm. This makes restorative justice uniquely suited to address the sensitive and intricate issues surrounding sexual abuse, as it places the well-being of survivors at the forefront and seeks to foster a path toward healing, accountability, and community support.

CHAPTER 3

SEXUAL ABUSE: PREVALENCE AND IMPACT

Statistics and Prevalence:

Sexual abuse is a distressing and widespread issue that affects individuals in every corner of the globe. While it often goes unreported due to stigma and shame, available data paints a grim picture of the scope and prevalence of this pervasive problem.

- According to the World Health Organization (WHO), approximately 1 in 3 women worldwide has experienced physical and/or sexual intimate partner violence or non-partner sexual violence in their lifetime.

- The statistics on child sexual abuse are equally concerning. The United Nations Children's Fund (UNICEF) reports that globally, 1 in 10 girls under the age of 18 has experienced forced sexual acts.

- It's important to note that sexual abuse affects people of all genders. The prevalence of sexual abuse in men and gender-diverse individuals is also a significant concern, though it is often underreported.

- In addition to intimate partner violence and child sexual abuse, sexual harassment in workplaces and public spaces is widespread. Numerous surveys and studies have highlighted the prevalence of sexual harassment and its impact on individuals' mental and emotional well-being.

Alarming Statistics and Urgency:

These statistics underscore the urgency of addressing sexual abuse. They reveal a troubling reality in which countless individuals are subjected to physical, emotional, and psychological harm. The true extent of the problem may be even higher, given that many cases go unreported due to fear, shame, and a lack of support.

Understanding the prevalence of sexual abuse is crucial for several reasons. It highlights the urgent need for preventative measures, support systems, and legal reforms. It underscores the importance of shifting from punitive justice systems to more holistic and victim-centered approaches, such as restorative justice, to address the deep trauma and societal impact of sexual abuse.

By shedding light on the prevalence of sexual abuse, we emphasize the imperative of raising awareness, providing resources for survivors, and working collectively to create a safer and more empathetic world—one where sexual abuse is not only condemned but actively prevented and addressed.

Psychological and Emotional Impact of Sexual Abuse

Sexual abuse inflicts profound psychological and emotional wounds on survivors, leaving scars that can last a lifetime. Understanding the devastating impact on the mental and emotional well-being of individuals is crucial:

1. Complex Trauma: Sexual abuse often results in complex trauma, which differs from single-incident trauma. It involves repeated violations of trust and boundaries, leading to deep and lasting emotional wounds. Survivors may

experience feelings of powerlessness, betrayal, and humiliation.

2. Fear: Survivors of sexual abuse often live in fear, both during and after the abuse. They may fear further victimization, have nightmares, and experience intense anxiety, making it challenging to feel safe in their own bodies and in the world around them.

3. Shame and Guilt: Survivors commonly experience overwhelming feelings of shame and guilt, even though they are not at fault for the abuse. They may blame themselves for the actions of the offender, contributing to a diminished sense of self-worth and self-esteem.

4. Depression and Anxiety: Sexual abuse frequently leads to depression and anxiety disorders. Survivors may struggle with persistent sadness, hopelessness, and constant worry. These conditions can have a debilitating impact on their daily lives.

5. Post-Traumatic Stress Disorder (PTSD): Many survivors develop PTSD, characterized by flashbacks, intrusive thoughts, and emotional numbing. These symptoms can persist for years and can be triggered by reminders of the abuse.

6. Dissociation: Survivors may use dissociation as a coping mechanism during the abuse, disconnecting from their own bodies to endure the trauma. This can lead to difficulties with memory, identity, and self-awareness.

7. Trust Issues: Sexual abuse erodes trust in others, making it challenging for survivors to form healthy relationships. They may struggle with intimacy and vulnerability, fearing that others will betray their trust.

8. Self-Harming Behaviors: Some survivors resort to self-harming behaviors, such as cutting or substance abuse, as a way to cope with emotional pain and regain a sense of control.

9. Impact on Sexuality: Sexual abuse can profoundly affect one's relationship with their own sexuality. Survivors may experience sexual dysfunction, low libido, or difficulties with intimacy.

10. Long-Term Consequences: The psychological consequences of sexual abuse can persist for years, even decades, if left unaddressed. Survivors may carry the emotional scars throughout their lives, impacting their overall well-being, relationships, and quality of life.

It is crucial to recognize that healing from sexual abuse is a complex and ongoing process. Survivors benefit from trauma-informed care, therapy, support networks, and, in some cases, restorative justice processes that acknowledge the profound psychological and emotional impact of sexual abuse and offer paths to recovery and resilience.

Societal Implications of Sexual Abuse:

The impact of sexual abuse is not confined to individual survivors; it has far-reaching societal implications that affect communities, institutions, and systems in profound ways:

1. Erosion of Trust in Interpersonal Relationships:

Sexual abuse can erode trust within families, friendships, and communities. Survivors may struggle to trust others, leading to difficulties in forming healthy and meaningful relationships. This erosion of trust can have a lasting impact on social bonds.

2. Undermining the Sense of Safety in Communities:

Communities can be deeply affected by the knowledge of sexual abuse cases within their midst. The revelation of such cases can shatter the perceived safety of neighborhoods and institutions, leaving community members feeling vulnerable and concerned for their loved ones.

3. Challenge to the Effectiveness of Justice Systems:

Sexual abuse cases often highlight shortcomings in the justice system. These may include barriers to reporting, difficulties in obtaining convictions, and challenges in providing adequate support to survivors during legal proceedings. Such issues can erode public confidence in the justice system's ability to address sexual abuse effectively.

4. Stigma and Silence:

Societal stigma and shame surrounding sexual abuse can deter survivors from coming forward to report their experiences. This silence perpetuates a culture where sexual abuse can thrive in secrecy, further challenging efforts to address and prevent it.

5. Perpetuation of Gender Inequality:

Sexual abuse, often rooted in power imbalances, perpetuates gender inequality. It reinforces harmful stereotypes and norms related to masculinity and femininity, which can have broader societal repercussions in terms of gender discrimination and violence.

6. Economic Consequences:

Sexual abuse can have economic consequences for both survivors and society as a whole. Survivors may face challenges in education and employment due to the emotional and psychological trauma they endure. Additionally, society bears the economic burden of addressing the healthcare and social service needs of survivors.

7. Societal Responsibility:

Addressing sexual abuse is a collective societal responsibility. It requires proactive efforts to create a safer and more supportive environment for survivors. This includes implementing prevention programs, supporting survivors in their healing journey, and advocating for legal reforms that prioritize victim-centered approaches, such as restorative justice.

8. Fostering a Culture of Prevention and Accountability:

Societal implications also encompass the need to foster a culture of prevention and accountability. Communities and institutions must actively work to prevent sexual abuse through education, awareness campaigns, and intervention programs. Holding offenders accountable for their actions is vital for creating a safer society.

In summary, sexual abuse's societal implications are extensive and multifaceted, affecting trust, safety, justice, and gender equality. Recognizing these implications highlights the collective responsibility to address sexual abuse, support survivors, and create a society where consent, respect, and safety are upheld as fundamental principles.

CHAPTER 4

CHILDHOOD SEXUAL ABUSE

The Secret Storm

"He lies in wait like a lion in cover; He lies in wait to catch the helpless; he catches the helpless and drags them off in his net."   (Psalm 10:9)

A victim of childhood sexual abuse is any boy or girl under age of 18 who has suffered one or more experiences of sexual abuse. Such abuse results in emotional, mental, spiritual, or physical harm.:

Childhood sexual abuse refers to any form of sexual activity that occurs between an adult or older adolescent and a child or younger adolescent, under the age of 18. This can include a wide range of behaviors, from touching or fondling to penetration or other sexual acts. Childhood sexual abuse is a traumatic experience that can have lasting physical, emotional, and psychological effects.

Many survivors of childhood sexual abuse struggle with feelings of shame, guilt, and self-blame. They may also experience symptoms of post-traumatic stress disorder (PTSD), such as flashbacks, nightmares, and anxiety.

Survivors may also have difficulty forming healthy relationships and trusting others.

It's important for survivors of childhood sexual abuse to know that they are not alone and that help is available. There are many resources available, including therapy, support groups, and hotlines, that can provide survivors with the tools and support they need to heal from their trauma. It's also important to report the abuse to the appropriate authorities and to seek medical attention if necessary.

If you suspect that a child is being sexually abused, it's important to take action to protect them. This may involve reporting the abuse to the authorities, providing support and resources to the child and their family, and working to prevent future abuse from occurring.

Any sexual abuse is a particularly sinister type of trauma because of the shame it instills in the victim. But with childhood sexual abuse, victims are often too young to know how to express what is happening and seek out help. When not properly treated, this can result in a lifetime of PTSD, depression and anxiety.

Incest is sexual interaction with a child or an adolescent by a person who is a member of the child's family - a blood relative, an adoptive relative, or someone related by marriage or remarriage.

The Bible is not silent about incest. Leviticus 18:6 says, 'No one is to approach any close relative to have sexual relations.

Some of the most startling statistics unearthed during research into sexual abuse are that children are three times as likely to be victims of rape than adults, and stranger abuse constitutes by far the minority of cases. It is more likely for a child to experience sexual abuse at the hands of a family member or another supposedly trustworthy adult.

Typically, childhood sexual abuse is not a one-time, isolated incident, but rather a premeditated plan, resulting in repeated abuse by the perpetrator. Perpetrators follow a typical pattern of behavior: first seduction, then stimulation, silence and suppression of the child. Once suppressed, the child loses all hope.:

According to childtrauma.org, in the U.S. one out of three females and one out of five males have been victims of sexual abuse before the age of 18 years. According to the American Academy of Experts in Traumatic Stress (AAETS), 30% of all male children are molested in some way, compared to 40% of females.

Below are the typical patterns of behavior followed by a child abuse perpetrator:

Seduction --- Stimulation --- Silence --- Suppression:

a) Silence - The perpetrator moves to ensure the victim's silence through intimidation and fear-inducing threats. Abusers are keenly aware of their power over innocent   prey.:

b) Stimulation - The child feels pleasure in physical touch that seems appropriate, affirming and warm. Over time the child becomes desensitized and vulnerable to the progression of more advanced sexual activity. By God's design, the body naturally responds to sexual stimulation.:

c) Suppression - The child, feeling no choice but to bow to the perpetrator because they feel alone and powerless slips quietly into emotional enslavement. When hopelessness reigns, the light in the child's soul is snuffed out.:

d) Seduction - The perpetrator plays on the child's emotions by developing intimacy, progressively building trust and giving pleasure; accomplished by giving gifts or money, or by being 'their friend'. (Psalm 36:1-4):

True - By God's design, it is natural for the body to respond to sexual stimulation. When a perpetrator advances sexual activity with a child, the increased physical encroachment may not be enjoyable for the child, but the increased sexual stimulation can be enjoyable and the child may feel conflicted over the mixture of pain and pleasure, which in turn causes guilt. No guilt should ever be attributed to the child, only to the abuser.:

Related to this, another legacy of sexual abuse is that children abused at any early age often become hyper-sexualized or sexually reactive. Issues with promiscuity is unfortunately a common reaction to childhood sexual abuse. Others who were sexually abused as children have experienced issues with sexual dysfunction and self-destructive behavior when they got older.

Although child abuse may be a one-time event or continue for years, over time, when the child gets older, they will usually tell someone.

When a child has no one to rescue them from the abusive relationship, they feel betrayed and hopeless of ever being saved by anyone, including God. What is 'snuffed out' within the spirit of the child when the soul is suppressed and the child has this hopelessness? The soul is suppressed and the light within the spirit is snuffed out.

After an act of sexual abuse, victimizers (perpetrators) fear being found out. They seek to shift the blame to the child (victim) by unloading guilt upon them and deceiving them. This strategy is used in the form of a game.:

Facing the truth that child abuse is taking place is the first step to healing:

What are the 'Do's and Don'ts of awareness' of child sexual abuse?

a) Do be aware that child abuse is a crime and must be reported.

b) Do be aware that children are usually abused by people they know.

c) Do be aware most often, physical abuse is violent, but sexual abuse may not be.:

d) Do be aware that children seldom lie about abuse.:

e) Do be aware that children may deny or change their stories because of fear.:

f) Do be aware that sexual abuse is progressive and will get worse if not stopped.:

g) Don't be in denial, no matter how difficult it is to believe what you hear.:

h) Don't assume that if happened only once, that it is not serious.:

i) Don't minimize the abuse.:

j) Don't let the offender go without confrontation.:

k) Don't blame other family members.:

l) Don't keep abuse a family secret.:

The first thing the Biblical Counselor should do first when child abuse is suspected is to seek the help of a professional who is trained to work with children.

Seeking the guidance of a trained professional when child abuse is suspected to: verify or relieve your suspicions

Abuse is sin. It doesn't matter if it's physical, emotional, verbal, sexual, or spiritual; it is all sin. Titus 2:4 says we are to love our children. And there is no place in such love for sexual abuse.

a) To verify or to relieve your suspicions.:

b) Further inform yourself (not in the presence of the child) (Proverbs 24:5-6):

Seeking the guidance of a trained professional when child abuse is suspected to verify or to relieve suspicions and to further inform yourself (not in the presence of the child). What might the biblical counselor do to verify or to relieve suspicions of child abuse and to gain further information? (Proverbs 24:5-6):

Contact a professional and/or a child advocacy program to discuss your concerns privately and to evaluate the child and make recommendations.

Contact a family attorney, a pastor or spiritual leader, a shelter for women and children and Child Protective Services.

Contact the police and the local district attorney's office.

It's crucial for every victim of sexual abuse to seek counseling. Since 35% of child sexual abusers were once abused themselves (higher in males), counseling might also help to reduce the possibility of a victim repeating the abusive pattern. And studies have also shown that children who experience sexual abuse tend to recover quicker and with better results if they have a supportive, caring adult (ideally a parent) consistently in their life.

What should the biblical counselor do if a child discloses sexual abuse?

If a child discloses sexual abuse to a biblical counselor, it's important to respond in a compassionate and supportive manner while also taking steps to ensure the child's safety. Here are some steps a biblical counselor can take:

1. Listen and believe the child: It's important to take the child's disclosure seriously and to believe them. Provide a safe and supportive environment for the child to share their story.

2. Reassure the child that they are not to blame: Many children who have experienced sexual abuse may feel responsible or ashamed. Make sure the child understands that the abuse was not their fault.

3. Report the abuse: It is mandatory in most states to report child sexual abuse to the authorities. Biblical counselors should comply with their state's laws on mandatory reporting of child abuse. In addition, the

counselor should follow any church or organizational policies regarding reporting.

4. Provide support and resources: The child may need additional support, such as medical care or counseling. The counselor can help the child and their family find appropriate resources.

5. Maintain confidentiality: While it's important to report the abuse to the appropriate authorities, it's also important to maintain the child's privacy and confidentiality as much as possible. Only share information on a need-to-know basis.

It's important for biblical counselors to receive appropriate training on responding to child sexual abuse and to have a plan in place for how to respond if a child discloses abuse.

a) Stay calm.:

b) Take time to sensitively answer any questions from the child.:

c) Be available to the child at all times.:

d) Remain with the child, or only leave the child with another adult with whom you and the child trust.:

e) Respect the privacy of the child from those who have a need to know.:

f) Make no promises you can't keep, such as: 'Your mom won't be angry'

g) Explain that law enforcement agencies must be informed and what will happen next.:

h) Be prepared to provide protection. arrange for a medical exam, and obtain professional counseling.:

What are practical action steps and follow-up that the biblical counselor can take if a child discloses sexual abuse?

a) Take the child to a pediatrician or to the local hospital emergency room for immediate examination and documentation.

b) Relate why you suspect possible child abuse and recommend that it be turned over to a caseworker.

c) Ask for a copy of medical records in writing, and copies of photographs if they are taken.

d) Keep a paper trail of all contacts you make.

e) Follow-up with caseworkers on a regular basis, asking about the status of the case and how you can be of assistance.

f) If a caseworker's file disappears, supply duplicates of your own records.

g) If the local services are not responsive, keep appealing to higher authority by contacting a State of Federal Agency. (1 Peter 2:13:14):

The ways to open the hearts of the victims and gently draw the child out into the light of the truth, breaking the power of the secret. (Proverbs 20:15):

a) Pray for supernatural wisdom from the Spirit of God.:

b) Provide a safe atmosphere, away from upsetting people and places.:

c) Ask, 'Have you been experiencing something uncomfortable or confusing?

d) Listen carefully, repeated what is said, and ask, 'Did I get it right?'

e) Be cautious about asking leading questions such as, 'Did he do xxxxx to you?

f) Let authorities with expertise in childhood sexual abuse ask most of the questions.:

g) Communicate that you believe the child.:

h) Acknowledge that the offender is wrong.:

i) Give assurance that the child is not to blame.:

j) Confirm that 'telling' is the right thing to do.:

k) Provide a safe atmosphere by displaying genuine love and compassion.:

Anyone who has been abused or who has abused children can find hope, healing, and forgiveness in Jesus Christ. Talking to a pastor or finding a faith-based counselor or a support group may be a good place to begin the journey to wholeness.

The role playing with the child to assert the child's ability to say 'no' to the perpetrator. This is suggested as a way to instill confidence and build assertiveness in a young heart and help the child to resist inappropriate sexual advances.

Role playing is a good way to teach a child to say no … not only to inappropriate sexual advances but also to other bad actions as well. Sometimes I have used puppets with young children. The puppet always comes tempting the child with wrong actions. It is important to always let the children play the part of the one who is strong and says "No.

In child abuse, what does the perpetrator's most powerful weapon and strategy?

In child abuse, the perpetrator's most powerful weapon and strategy is secrecy. By keeping the abuse hidden, the perpetrator maintains power and control over the child and can continue the abuse without fear of consequences.

Perpetrators of child abuse often use a variety of tactics to keep the abuse a secret, including threats, manipulation, and coercion. They may tell the child that the abuse is a "secret" or that it is their fault, which can cause the child to feel ashamed or guilty about what is happening to them. The perpetrator may also use their position of authority or trust to keep the abuse hidden, such as by telling the child not to tell anyone or by warning them of the consequences if they do.

It's important to remember that the responsibility for the abuse lies solely with the perpetrator, and that children who have experienced abuse are not to blame. By breaking the cycle of secrecy and reporting the abuse to the appropriate authorities, we can help protect children from further harm and hold perpetrators accountable for their actions.

It is imperative to know that, people who abuse children may offer a combination of gifts or treats and threats about what will happen if the child says "o" or tells someone. They may scare the child with threats of being hurt physically, but more often the threat is about what will be lost if they tell – such as the family breaking up or someone going to prison.

In order to keep the abuse a secret, the abuser will often play on the child's fear, embarrassment or guilt about what is happening, perhaps convincing them that no one will believe them or that the child will be punished. Sometimes the abuser will convince the child that he or she enjoyed it and wanted it to happen.

In child abuse, the God's strategy is?

God's strategy in addressing child abuse is one of love, compassion, and justice. Scripture teaches that children are precious in God's sight and that God has a special concern for their welfare. In Matthew 18:6, Jesus says, "If anyone causes one of these little ones—those who believe in me—to stumble, it would be better for them to have a large millstone hung around their neck and to be drowned in the depths of the sea."

God's love and compassion for children are also evident in the many verses that speak to caring for and protecting the vulnerable. For example, in Psalm 82:3-4, God commands us to "defend the weak and the fatherless; uphold the cause of the poor and the oppressed. Rescue the weak and the needy; deliver them from the hand of the wicked."

In terms of justice, God is a God of righteousness and holds all people accountable for their actions. In Deuteronomy 32:4, it says, "He is the Rock, his works are perfect, and all his ways are just. A faithful God who does no wrong, upright and just is he." Those who harm children will ultimately face God's judgment.

As biblical counselors, we can follow God's example by showing love and compassion to children who have experienced abuse, speaking out against injustice, and working to protect the vulnerable. We can also pray for those who have been harmed and for those who perpetrate abuse, that they may turn to God and seek forgiveness and healing.

Children have a special place in God's heart and anyone who harms a child is inviting God's wrath upon himself. When Jesus' disciples tried to keep children from coming to Jesus, He rebuked them and welcomed the children to His side, saying, "Let the little children come to me and do not hinder them for the kingdom of God belongs to such as these" (Mark 10:14). Then He took the children in His arms and blessed them (verse 16). The Bible promotes child blessing, not child abuse.

CHAPTER 5

THE TRAUMA OF SURVIVORS

The trauma experienced by survivors of sexual abuse is a deeply complex and distressing phenomenon. It encompasses a range of psychological and emotional responses to the abuse and its aftermath. Here's why understanding trauma is imperative:

Understanding Trauma:

- Psychological and Emotional Impact: Survivors of sexual abuse often experience a profound psychological and emotional impact. This can include symptoms of post-traumatic stress disorder (PTSD), such as flashbacks, nightmares, and heightened anxiety. It may also involve depression, anxiety disorders, and dissociation.

- Emotional Distress: Survivors frequently grapple with a myriad of intense emotions, including fear, anger, shame, guilt, and a sense of powerlessness. These emotions can be overwhelming and may persist for years or even a lifetime.

- Complex Trauma: Sexual abuse is a form of complex trauma, characterized by repeated and prolonged exposure to traumatic events. It differs from single-incident trauma and can result in deep and lasting emotional wounds.

- Challenges in Coping: Survivors may employ various coping mechanisms to deal with the emotional pain, including self-harming behaviors, substance abuse, or avoidance. These strategies can be detrimental to their well-being.

- Impact on Relationships: Trauma can profoundly affect survivors' relationships with others. Trust issues, difficulties with intimacy, and feelings of isolation are common challenges faced by survivors.

- Barriers to Disclosure: The trauma of sexual abuse often contributes to barriers in disclosing the abuse. Survivors may fear judgment, stigma, retaliation, or disbelief, preventing them from seeking help or justice.

Why Understanding Trauma is Imperative:

Understanding trauma is crucial for several reasons:

- Empathy and Support: A deep understanding of trauma allows individuals and institutions to offer survivors the empathy and support they need. It helps in creating a safe and nonjudgmental environment where survivors feel heard and validated.

- Trauma-Informed Care: Knowledge of trauma is fundamental for trauma-informed care—a compassionate and informed approach to assisting survivors. Trauma-informed care recognizes the effects of trauma on individuals and prioritizes their well-being.

- Tailored Interventions: Understanding the intricacies of trauma allows for tailored interventions and therapies that address survivors' specific needs. Trauma-informed therapies aim to minimize retraumatization and promote healing.

- Breaking the Silence: Understanding trauma contributes to breaking the silence surrounding sexual abuse. It encourages survivors to come forward, seek help, and access resources for their recovery.

- Promoting Healing: Ultimately, understanding trauma is essential for promoting healing and resilience among survivors. It acknowledges the profound challenges they face and emphasizes the importance of a victim-centered, trauma-informed approach to justice and support.

By embarking on a journey into the intricate landscape of trauma experienced by survivors of sexual abuse, we pave the way for more empathetic and effective responses that prioritize healing and recovery.

Trauma-Informed Care:

Trauma-informed care is an approach to providing support and services that recognizes and responds to the impact of trauma on individuals' lives. It is a cornerstone in the process of assisting survivors on their path to recovery. The principles of trauma-informed care emphasize the importance of creating safe and supportive environments that acknowledge the impact of trauma. Here are the key principles:

1. Safety: Ensuring physical and emotional safety is paramount in trauma-informed care. Creating an environment where survivors feel safe and secure is the foundation of the approach.

2. Trustworthiness and Transparency: Building trust is crucial. Individuals and institutions must be honest, transparent, and reliable in their interactions with survivors. Consistency and clear communication are key.

3. Peer Support: Peer support, where survivors can connect with others who have experienced trauma, can be a valuable part of the healing journey. Peer support offers a sense of belonging and validation.

4. Collaboration and Mutuality: Trauma-informed care is collaborative. It involves a partnership between survivors and service providers, with the survivor's voice and choice being central in decision-making.

5. Empowerment, Voice, and Choice: Empowering survivors to make choices and have a say in their care is essential. This empowers them to regain a sense of control over their lives.

6. Cultural, Historical, and Gender Sensitivity: Recognizing and respecting cultural, historical, and gender-related factors that impact the survivor's experience is critical. Trauma-informed care must be culturally sensitive and avoid retraumatization.

7. Understanding the Impact of Trauma: Service providers should have an understanding of the impact of trauma on individuals' lives, including the potential for complex trauma and its long-lasting effects.

8. Resilience and Strengths-Based: Trauma-informed care acknowledges the resilience and strengths of survivors. It focuses on building on these strengths to support recovery.

9. Trauma-Informed Practices: Institutions and individuals should adopt trauma-informed practices in all aspects of care, from intake procedures to treatment modalities. This includes avoiding practices that may inadvertently retraumatize survivors.

10. Social, Emotional, and Physical Well-Being: Trauma-informed care recognizes the interconnectedness of social, emotional, and physical well-being. It addresses not only immediate needs but also the long-term recovery and well-being of survivors.

By adopting trauma-informed approaches, individuals and institutions can better assist survivors in their healing journey. These principles guide the provision of services, therapy, and support in a way that respects survivors' experiences, fosters trust, and promotes healing and recovery.

Barriers to Disclosure:

Survivors of sexual abuse often encounter numerous barriers when contemplating whether to disclose their experiences. These barriers can be significant and may deter survivors from coming forward. Recognizing and addressing these barriers is essential to create a supportive environment for survivors to seek help and support when they are ready. Here are some of the key barriers:

1. Stigma and Shame: One of the most significant barriers to disclosure is the stigma associated with sexual abuse. Survivors often fear being judged or blamed for the abuse. They may carry a deep sense of shame, which can prevent them from speaking out.

2. Fear of Retaliation: Survivors may fear retaliation from the perpetrator, especially if the abuser is someone known to them or in a position of power. This fear can be a powerful deterrent to disclosure.

3. Lack of Trust: Many survivors struggle with trust issues, both due to the betrayal they experienced during the abuse and fears of not being believed or taken seriously if they disclose.

4. Minimizing the Experience: Some survivors may minimize or deny the severity of the abuse, believing that it wasn't "bad enough" to warrant disclosure. This can be a form of self-protection or a result of minimizing reactions from others.

5. Isolation: Sexual abuse often leaves survivors feeling isolated and alone. They may not have a support network to turn to, which can make disclosure even more challenging.

6. Fear of Legal Proceedings: The legal process can be daunting for survivors. Fear of facing the abuser in court, invasive questioning, and concerns about the outcome can discourage disclosure.

7. Cultural and Religious Factors: Cultural norms and religious beliefs can influence a survivor's decision to disclose. Some cultures stigmatize survivors, and religious beliefs may discourage discussing sexual abuse.

8. Lack of Information: Survivors may not have access to information about resources and support available to them. This lack of knowledge can prevent them from seeking help.

9. Age and Developmental Stage: Age and developmental stage can impact a survivor's ability to disclose. Children may not have the language or understanding to communicate their experiences, and teenagers may fear repercussions from parents or caregivers.

10. Mental Health and Coping Mechanisms: Some survivors cope with the trauma of sexual abuse by repressing memories or using avoidance as a coping mechanism. This can make it difficult to acknowledge and disclose the abuse.

11. Perceived Lack of Support: Survivors who have seen others come forward and face negative consequences may perceive a lack of support or justice, further discouraging disclosure.

By recognizing and addressing these barriers to disclosure, society can create a more compassionate and supportive environment for survivors. This includes reducing stigma, ensuring access to resources, providing trauma-informed care, and fostering a culture where survivors are believed, respected, and empowered to seek help when they are ready.

CHAPTER 6

TRADITIONAL CRIMINAL JUSTICE RESPONSES

Traditional criminal justice responses to sexual abuse cases typically involve the investigation and prosecution of offenders through the criminal justice system. This process centers on criminal trials and can include various stages such as reporting the abuse, police investigations, legal proceedings, and sentencing. However, these responses have inherent limitations when applied to sexual abuse cases:

Criminal Trials and Their Limitations:

1. Burden of Proof: Criminal trials place a significant burden of proof on the prosecution, requiring them to prove the defendant's guilt beyond a reasonable doubt. This high standard can be difficult to meet in cases where evidence may be scarce or when the abuse occurred in private without witnesses.

2. Retraumatization of Survivors: The adversarial nature of criminal trials can retraumatize survivors. They may be subjected to intense questioning by defense attorneys,

reliving the traumatic experience in court, and facing skepticism or victim-blaming.

3. Focus on Punishment: Traditional criminal justice systems primarily focus on punishment as a means of retribution and deterrence. While punishment is essential in some cases, it may not address the root causes of sexual abuse or support survivors in their healing journey.

4. Long Legal Processes: Legal proceedings in sexual abuse cases can be lengthy and emotionally draining for survivors. This extended process can deter survivors from seeking justice and can exacerbate their trauma.

5. Limited Support for Survivors: The criminal justice system often lacks comprehensive support services for survivors. While some resources exist, they may not adequately address survivors' emotional, psychological, and practical needs.

6. Low Reporting Rates: Due to the challenges and limitations of the criminal justice system, sexual abuse cases often go unreported. Many survivors fear the legal process and the potential repercussions of disclosing their experiences.

7. Focus on Offender Accountability: While offender accountability is crucial, the singular focus on punishing offenders may not address the complex needs of survivors, including their healing, recovery, and long-term well-being.

8. Limited Restitution and Restoration: Traditional criminal justice systems are often ill-equipped to facilitate restitution and restoration between survivors and offenders, leaving survivors without opportunities for closure or reconciliation.

These limitations highlight the need for alternative approaches to addressing sexual abuse cases, such as restorative justice, which prioritize healing, accountability, and the restoration of survivors' lives. Restorative justice offers a victim-centered and trauma-informed approach that can address the unique challenges posed by sexual abuse cases and better support survivors on their path to recovery.

Victim's Experience within the Justice System:

The journey survivors of sexual abuse face within the criminal justice system can be fraught with challenges and emotional turmoil. Here, we delve into the victim's experience, including their interactions with law enforcement, legal proceedings, and courtroom experiences:

1. Reporting to Law Enforcement: For many survivors, the process begins with reporting the abuse to law enforcement. This step can be intimidating, and survivors may fear being disbelieved, judged, or blamed.

2. Investigation: Survivors may have to recount their traumatic experiences multiple times during the investigation process, which can be emotionally exhausting. They might also have to provide evidence, such as medical records or forensic examinations.

3. Legal Proceedings: Legal proceedings, including pre-trial hearings and the trial itself, can be long and emotionally taxing. Survivors may be required to testify in court, facing cross-examination by defense attorneys, which can be retraumatizing.

4. Courtroom Atmosphere: The adversarial nature of criminal trials can create a hostile and intimidating courtroom atmosphere. Survivors may feel overwhelmed, vulnerable, and unsupported.

5. Lack of Support: Survivors often report feeling isolated within the legal system. They may not receive adequate emotional or psychological support during the process, exacerbating their trauma.

6. Impact on Emotional and Psychological Well-Being: The entire journey within the justice system can take a toll on survivors' emotional and psychological well-being.

Anxiety, depression, and post-traumatic stress symptoms may intensify.

7. Secondary Victimization: Survivors may experience secondary victimization, where they feel revictimized by the very system meant to bring them justice. This can occur through insensitive or judgmental interactions with law enforcement, legal professionals, or court personnel.

8. Outcome Uncertainty: The outcome of the trial is often uncertain, and survivors may face disappointment or frustration if the case does not result in a conviction or if the sentence is perceived as inadequate.

9. Long-Term Impact: The emotional scars from the legal process can persist long after the trial concludes. Survivors may struggle with trust issues, fear of retaliation, and difficulty in forming healthy relationships.

The Need for a Victim-Centered Approach:

The challenging journey survivors face within the criminal justice system underscores the need for a more victim-centered approach. Such an approach places the well-being and needs of survivors at the forefront. It involves providing comprehensive support services, trauma-informed care, and recognizing the profound emotional and psychological impact of the legal process. A victim-centered approach seeks to minimize retraumatization and empower survivors on their path to healing and recovery.

Unresolved Trauma:

The issue of unresolved trauma within the traditional criminal justice system is a critical concern. Even after the conclusion of a trial, survivors of sexual abuse may still carry the weight of trauma, and this unresolved trauma can have long-lasting effects on their lives. Here's why this issue is significant:

1. Impact on Healing: The legal process, with its focus on prosecution and punishment, may not adequately address survivors' emotional and psychological healing. Survivors may

still grapple with feelings of fear, shame, and guilt long after the trial ends.

2. Retraumatization: The adversarial nature of criminal trials can retraumatize survivors, as they are subjected to intense scrutiny and cross-examination. This retraumatization can exacerbate their emotional wounds.

3. Legal Outcomes: The outcome of a trial, whether it results in a conviction or acquittal, may not provide closure for survivors. They may continue to struggle with unresolved questions and emotions related to their experiences.

4. Trust and Safety: Unresolved trauma can erode survivors' trust in others and their sense of safety. They may find it difficult to form healthy relationships or feel secure in their daily lives.

5. Long-Term Effects: The effects of unresolved trauma can persist for years or even a lifetime. Survivors may experience symptoms of post-traumatic stress disorder (PTSD), depression, anxiety, and other mental health challenges.

6. Preventing Disclosure: The fear of unresolved trauma may deter survivors from reporting abuse or seeking help within the legal system. This can perpetuate a culture of silence around sexual abuse.

7. Need for Alternative Approaches: Recognizing the limitations of the traditional criminal justice system in addressing unresolved trauma highlights the need for alternative approaches. Restorative justice, as explored in subsequent chapters, offers a different paradigm that prioritizes healing, accountability, and the restoration of survivors' lives.

In exploring the issue of unresolved trauma, we acknowledge the importance of a more holistic and victim-centered approach to justice and support. Addressing unresolved trauma requires not only accountability for offenders but also comprehensive care and resources for survivors, with a focus on their well-being and recovery. Restorative justice, as an alternative approach, seeks to meet these critical needs and provides a pathway to address the long-lasting effects of trauma.

CHAPTER 7

INTRODUCTION TO RESTORATIVE JUSTICE FOR SEXUAL ABUSE

Restorative justice represents a paradigm shift in our approach to addressing the deeply complex and sensitive issue of sexual abuse. Unlike the traditional criminal justice system, which often focuses on punishment and legal processes, restorative justice places the healing and well-being of survivors at its core. This chapter serves as an introduction to the transformative potential of restorative justice within the context of sexual abuse cases.

Core Concepts and Principles:

At the heart of restorative justice lie several core concepts and principles that distinguish it from the conventional criminal justice system. These principles include:

1. Accountability: Restorative justice seeks to hold offenders accountable for their actions, not solely through punitive measures, but by fostering a genuine understanding of the harm they've caused and a commitment to making amends.

2. Empathy: Central to restorative justice is the cultivation of empathy. It encourages dialogue between survivors and offenders, fostering a deeper understanding of each other's experiences and emotions.

3. Restoration of Relationships: Unlike the adversarial nature of criminal trials, restorative justice aims to restore damaged relationships. It recognizes that sexual abuse affects not only the survivor and offender but also the broader community, and it seeks to rebuild trust and connections.

4. Healing-Centered: Restorative justice prioritizes the healing and well-being of survivors. It acknowledges the emotional and psychological trauma caused by sexual abuse and seeks to provide the necessary support for recovery.

5. Community Involvement: Restorative justice extends beyond the survivor and offender to involve the broader community. It recognizes that sexual abuse has ripple effects and strives to address the collective impact.

6. Voluntary Participation: Participation in restorative justice processes is voluntary, ensuring that survivors and offenders have agency in their decisions and a sense of control over the outcomes.

Understanding these core concepts and principles sets the stage for exploring how restorative justice can offer an alternative path to justice and recovery for survivors of sexual abuse. By emphasizing accountability, empathy, and the restoration of relationships, restorative justice aims to address the unique needs of survivors while holding offenders responsible for their actions in a more holistic and healing-focused manner.

Case Studies of Successful Restorative Approaches:

1. The S.A.F.E. Program (Sexual Abuse Family Education): In a community-based restorative justice program, survivors of sexual abuse, their families, and the offenders voluntarily participate in a facilitated process. This program incorporates therapy, education, and mediation to

address the needs of all parties involved. Through open dialogue, survivors have the opportunity to express their emotions and have their questions answered, offenders gain insight into the harm they've caused, and families receive support in rebuilding trust and relationships. The S.A.F.E. program exemplifies how restorative justice can foster healing, understanding, and rehabilitation within the family unit.

2. Circle Sentencing in Indigenous Communities: In some Indigenous communities, restorative justice practices have been integrated into the criminal justice system. Circle sentencing involves community members, survivors, offenders, and Elders coming together to discuss the impact of sexual abuse and determine appropriate resolutions. These circles emphasize healing, accountability, and reconciliation. By involving the community and acknowledging cultural values, this approach has shown success in addressing sexual abuse while promoting cultural healing and reintegration.

3. Restorative Justice in Educational Settings: Educational institutions have implemented restorative justice practices to address incidents of sexual abuse among students. In one case study, a restorative justice coordinator facilitated dialogues between survivors and offenders within a school setting. These dialogues focused on understanding the harm caused, making amends, and preventing future incidents. This approach not only supported survivors' healing but also provided an educational opportunity for offenders to learn from their actions and grow.

4. The Restorative Justice Project for Incarcerated Offenders: Some restorative justice initiatives extend to incarcerated offenders who have committed sexual abuse. In this case study, a program was designed to offer therapy and counseling to incarcerated offenders, encouraging them to take responsibility for their actions and develop empathy for

survivors. The program aimed to reduce recidivism while addressing the emotional and psychological needs of survivors.

These case studies underscore the effectiveness of restorative justice in sexual abuse cases by demonstrating its capacity to address the needs of survivors, hold offenders accountable, and promote healing and reconciliation. They serve as practical examples of how restorative justice principles can be applied in diverse settings, emphasizing the transformative potential of this approach in the context of sexual abuse.

CHAPTER 8

THE ROLE OF STAKEHOLDERS

The role of stakeholders is pivotal in the success of restorative justice processes for sexual abuse cases. These stakeholders include facilitators, survivors, offenders, and communities, each with unique responsibilities and perspectives:

1. Facilitators: Facilitators are trained professionals who guide the restorative justice process. They play a crucial role in creating a safe and structured environment for dialogue between survivors and offenders. Facilitators ensure that the process is respectful, empathetic, and focused on healing and resolution. They help participants understand the impact of the abuse, explore the harm caused, and work toward agreements that promote accountability and reconciliation.

2. Survivors: Survivors of sexual abuse are at the center of the restorative justice process. Their role involves sharing their experiences, expressing their feelings and needs, and actively participating in discussions about the harm caused. Survivors seek healing, validation, and an opportunity to be heard and acknowledged. They may also play a role in

shaping agreements that address their specific needs for support and restitution.

3. Offenders: Offenders in restorative justice processes are encouraged to take responsibility for their actions. They must listen to the survivors, acknowledge the harm caused, and express genuine remorse. Offenders may be required to make amends, either through direct actions, such as apologies or restitution, or through commitments to personal growth and rehabilitation. The goal is to help offenders understand the impact of their actions and actively work toward preventing further harm.

4. Communities: Communities serve as a critical support system within the restorative justice framework. They provide the context for healing and reconciliation. Communities may include family members, friends, advocates, and professionals who offer emotional and practical support to survivors and offenders. Their role is to create a network of care and accountability that reinforces the principles of restorative justice.

The involvement and collaboration of these stakeholders are essential for the restorative justice process to be effective. By recognizing the responsibilities and perspectives of each stakeholder, restorative justice approaches sexual abuse cases with a holistic and victim-centered perspective, aiming to address the unique needs of survivors, foster offender accountability, and promote healing and reconciliation within the broader community.

Why it is Important to Build Trust and Collaboration:

Building trust and fostering collaboration among stakeholders is of paramount importance in the context of restorative justice for sexual abuse cases. Here's why:

1. Safe and Supportive Environment: Trust is the foundation of any restorative justice process. Survivors, offenders, and facilitators must feel safe to engage in open and honest dialogue. Building trust creates an environment

where participants can share their experiences, express their emotions, and work toward resolution without fear of judgment or retaliation.

2. Effective Communication: Collaboration relies on effective communication. Trust enables survivors to communicate their needs, expectations, and boundaries clearly. It allows offenders to express genuine remorse and commitment to change. Facilitators can guide the process with empathy and sensitivity. Trust ensures that the dialogue remains productive and respectful.

3. Emotional Healing: Sexual abuse cases involve deep emotional wounds. Trusting relationships among stakeholders can be a source of emotional healing for survivors. Knowing that their voices are heard and their experiences are validated can contribute to their psychological well-being and recovery.

4. Accountability: Trust is essential for holding offenders accountable. Offenders are more likely to take responsibility for their actions and engage in meaningful amends when they trust that the process is fair and focused on healing rather than retribution.

5. Community Support: Communities play a crucial role in providing support and understanding. Trust within the community ensures that survivors and offenders receive the necessary resources and assistance. It reinforces the idea that sexual abuse is a collective concern that requires a collective response.

6. Sensitivity to Complexity: Sexual abuse cases are complex and sensitive. Building trust acknowledges this complexity and demonstrates a commitment to navigating it with care and empathy. It recognizes that survivors, offenders, and facilitators may have unique perspectives and needs.

7. Inclusivity: Trust and collaboration promote inclusivity. They ensure that all voices are heard and respected, regardless of background, identity, or role within the process. Inclusivity reinforces the idea that everyone has a stake in achieving healing and accountability.

8. Collective Effort: Sexual abuse cases require a collective effort from all stakeholders. Trust and collaboration emphasize that healing and accountability are not the sole responsibilities of one party but a shared endeavor. The interconnectedness of stakeholders highlights the need for cooperation and mutual support.

In summary, building trust and fostering collaboration create the necessary conditions for restorative justice to be effective in sexual abuse cases. These principles recognize the sensitivity of the issues involved and prioritize the creation of safe, supportive, and inclusive spaces for dialogue and resolution. Trust and collaboration are essential for achieving healing and accountability in these complex and emotionally charged cases.

CHAPTER 9

PREPARING FOR A RESTORATIVE PROCESS AND ITS IMPORTANCE

Preparing for a restorative process is a critical step in the restorative justice framework, especially in cases involving sexual abuse. It involves assessing the readiness and suitability of participants, obtaining informed consent, and implementing safety measures. This preparation is crucial for several reasons:

1. Emotional and Psychological Well-Being: Sexual abuse cases are emotionally and psychologically sensitive. Preparing participants ensures that they are emotionally ready to engage in the process without experiencing undue distress or harm.

2. Voluntary Participation: Assessing readiness ensures that participants willingly and voluntarily choose to participate, rather than feeling coerced or pressured into it. Informed consent is a fundamental ethical principle in restorative justice.

3. Safety: Safety measures are essential to protect the physical and emotional well-being of all participants. This

includes risk assessment and crisis management plans to address potential safety concerns.

4. Effectiveness: A well-prepared restorative process is more likely to be effective in achieving its goals, including healing, accountability, and reconciliation. Assessing readiness helps tailor the process to participants' needs.

Initial Assessments:

Initial assessments involve evaluating the readiness and suitability of participants for the restorative justice process. This assessment considers factors such as emotional preparedness, safety concerns, and the informed consent of all parties involved, including survivors and offenders. Here are some key aspects of initial assessments:

1. Emotional Readiness: Assess whether participants are emotionally prepared to engage in the process. This includes understanding their current emotional state and evaluating whether they can participate without experiencing undue harm.

2. Informed Consent: Ensure that participants fully understand the restorative justice process, their rights, and their roles. Informed consent should be voluntary, free from coercion, and obtained from all participants.

3. Safety Concerns: Identify any potential safety concerns, such as the risk of retraumatization or conflict escalation, and develop plans to address them.

4. Support Systems: Assess the availability of support systems for participants, including emotional support, legal counsel, or counseling services.

5. Cultural Considerations: Consider cultural factors and sensitivities that may influence the readiness of participants and the dynamics of the process.

6. Tailoring the Process: Based on the assessments, tailor the restorative process to meet the unique needs and circumstances of the participants.

In summary, initial assessments are essential to ensure that the restorative justice process is safe, ethical, and tailored to the emotional and psychological well-being of survivors and offenders. It establishes the foundation for a restorative process that respects the principles of voluntariness, informed consent, and safety, especially in the context of sexual abuse cases.

Informed Consent:

Informed consent is a foundational ethical principle in restorative justice. It is a process by which participants fully understand the restorative justice process, their rights, and their roles before choosing to participate. In the context of sexual abuse cases, where sensitivity and potential vulnerability are high, informed consent takes on particular importance. Here are key principles related to informed consent:

1. Voluntary Participation: Participants must choose to engage in the restorative justice process voluntarily, free from any form of coercion or pressure. They have the right to decline participation or withdraw at any point without repercussions.

2. Understanding the Process: Participants should receive clear and comprehensive information about what the restorative justice process entails, including its goals, procedures, and potential outcomes. This information helps participants make informed decisions about whether to participate.

3. Rights and Roles: Participants should be informed of their rights within the process, such as the right to be heard, the right to have a support person present, and the right to set boundaries. They should also understand their roles, responsibilities, and expectations.

4. Safety Measures: Information about safety measures and risk assessments should be provided to participants,

addressing potential concerns related to their emotional well-being and physical safety.

5. Privacy and Confidentiality: Participants should be aware of the confidentiality practices within the restorative justice process, including what information will be kept private and what may be shared with others, such as facilitators or support personnel.

6. Cultural Sensitivity: Informed consent should respect cultural diversity and sensitivities. Participants from different cultural backgrounds may have specific concerns or expectations related to the process.

7. Opportunity for Questions: Participants should have the opportunity to ask questions and seek clarification about any aspect of the process before providing their consent.

8. Time for Reflection: Participants should not be rushed into giving their consent. They should have adequate time to consider their decision, consult with support persons, or seek legal advice if necessary.

Informed consent ensures that participants enter the restorative justice process with a clear understanding of what to expect, the protections in place, and the freedom to choose their level of involvement. It upholds principles of autonomy, respect, and dignity, allowing survivors and offenders to make informed decisions about their participation in a process that can be emotionally challenging and transformative.

Why Safety Measures are Important:

Safety measures are of utmost importance in restorative justice processes, especially in cases involving sexual abuse. Here's why they are crucial:

1. Protection from Harm: Safety measures are designed to protect all participants from physical and emotional harm. In cases of sexual abuse, survivors may already be dealing with trauma, and safety measures help prevent retraumatization during the restorative process.

2. Emotional Well-Being: Sexual abuse cases can be emotionally charged and distressing. Safety measures ensure that participants' emotional well-being is safeguarded by creating a supportive and non-threatening environment for dialogue.

3. Risk Assessment: Conducting risk assessments helps identify potential safety concerns, such as the risk of conflict escalation, retaliation, or the exacerbation of emotional distress. Addressing these risks proactively minimizes potential harm.

4. Support Systems: Safety measures include access to support systems for participants. Survivors and offenders may require emotional support, legal counsel, or counseling services throughout the process. Knowing that these support systems are in place can increase participants' sense of security.

5. Crisis Management: In the event that a crisis or safety issue arises during the restorative process, having crisis management plans in place ensures a timely and effective response. This can include de-escalation strategies and mechanisms for temporarily suspending the process if necessary.

6. Community and Public Safety: Restorative justice processes can impact the broader community. Safety measures help maintain community safety by addressing concerns related to potential conflicts or disturbances that may arise from the process.

7. Facilitator Safety: Facilitators who guide the restorative process also require protection. Safety measures ensure that facilitators can work in a secure environment and are trained to handle potentially challenging situations.

8. Building Trust: Demonstrating a commitment to safety builds trust among participants. Knowing that their

safety is a priority helps survivors and offenders feel more comfortable engaging in the process.

9. Process Effectiveness: A safe and secure environment fosters more productive and meaningful dialogue. Participants are more likely to engage openly, express their feelings and needs, and work toward resolution when they feel protected.

In summary, safety measures are essential to create a secure, supportive, and inclusive space for restorative justice processes, particularly in cases as sensitive as sexual abuse. These measures not only protect participants but also contribute to the overall effectiveness of the process by promoting trust, healing, and accountability.

CHAPTER 10

THE RESTORATIVE DIALOGUE

The restorative dialogue is a central component of restorative justice processes. It is a structured and facilitated conversation that brings together survivors and offenders, along with support persons or facilitators, when necessary, to address the harm caused by the offense, explore the impact on all parties involved, and work toward resolution, healing, and accountability.

Why Restorative Dialogue is Important:

Restorative dialogue is important for several reasons:

1. Healing and Closure: It provides survivors with an opportunity to express their feelings, needs, and expectations, contributing to their healing and closure.

2. Offender Accountability: It encourages offenders to take responsibility for their actions, understand the harm they've caused, and make amends.

3. Communication and Understanding: It fosters open and empathetic communication between survivors and offenders, promoting mutual understanding and empathy.

4. Resolution: It aims to reach agreements or resolutions that address the harm and the needs of survivors, while also holding offenders accountable.

5. Community Involvement: It involves the broader community, emphasizing that sexual abuse is not only an issue between survivors and offenders but also a concern for the community as a whole.

Who Arranges the Restorative Dialogue:

Restorative dialogues are typically arranged and facilitated by trained professionals known as facilitators or restorative justice practitioners. Facilitators guide the process, ensure its structure and safety, and help participants communicate effectively. They play a crucial role in creating a safe and supportive environment for the dialogue.

Why Creating a Safe Space is Important:

Creating a safe space for the restorative dialogue is essential for several reasons:

1. Emotional Safety: Survivors and offenders may be dealing with trauma, guilt, or fear. Emotional safety ensures that participants can express themselves without feeling threatened or judged.

2. Trust: A safe space builds trust among participants, encouraging open and honest communication.

3. Confidentiality: Participants need to know that what is shared in the dialogue will be treated confidentially, fostering trust and a sense of security.

4. Effective Communication: Emotional safety is conducive to effective communication. It helps participants express their feelings, needs, and perspectives clearly.

5. Encouraging Participation: A safe space encourages active participation, as participants are more likely to engage when they feel comfortable and supported.

6. Resolution and Healing: Emotional safety contributes to the effectiveness of the restorative dialogue,

making it more likely to lead to resolution, healing, and accountability.

In summary, creating a safe and supportive environment for the restorative dialogue is a fundamental aspect of restorative justice. It ensures that survivors and offenders can engage in a constructive and empathetic conversation that addresses the harm caused and promotes healing and accountability. Facilitators play a crucial role in establishing and maintaining this safe space.

Why Communication Techniques are Important in Restorative Justice:

Effective communication is vital in restorative justice processes for several compelling reasons:

1. Facilitating Understanding: Communication techniques help participants understand each other's perspectives, feelings, and needs. This understanding is crucial for achieving empathy and reconciliation.

2. Promoting Accountability: Effective communication allows offenders to express genuine remorse and take responsibility for their actions. It also enables survivors to articulate the impact of the harm they've experienced.

3. Encouraging Openness: Restorative justice relies on open and honest dialogue. Communication techniques create an environment where participants feel safe to express themselves without fear of judgment or retaliation.

4. Conflict Resolution: Communication techniques, such as active listening and non-violent communication, can de-escalate conflicts and tensions during the dialogue, making it more likely to reach a resolution.

5. Empathy Building: Techniques like active listening and restorative language foster empathy among participants. When survivors and offenders truly listen to each other, they can better understand the emotional impact of the offense.

6. Effective Facilitation: Facilitators use communication techniques to guide the dialogue, ensure that it remains focused and respectful, and help participants express themselves clearly.

Communication Techniques in Restorative Justice:

Several communication techniques are particularly important in restorative justice:

1. Active Listening: Active listening involves giving full attention to the speaker, showing empathy, and asking clarifying questions. It ensures that participants feel heard and validated.

2. Non-Violent Communication (NVC): NVC is a communication model that encourages expressing feelings and needs honestly and without judgment. It promotes empathy, reduces defensiveness, and fosters understanding.

3. Restorative Language: Restorative language emphasizes using words that promote healing, accountability, and reconciliation. It avoids blaming language and encourages participants to take responsibility for their actions.

4. Reflective Responses: Reflective responses involve paraphrasing or summarizing what the speaker has said. It helps clarify understanding and shows respect for the speaker's perspective.

5. Asking Open-Ended Questions: Open-ended questions encourage participants to share more about their experiences and feelings. They invite deeper exploration of the issues at hand.

By incorporating these communication techniques, restorative justice processes can be more effective in achieving their goals of healing, accountability, and reconciliation. They create an environment where survivors and offenders can engage in meaningful dialogue that promotes understanding and connection, ultimately contributing to the resolution of harm caused by sexual abuse.

Encouraging Empathy and Accountability:

Encouraging empathy and accountability is a core objective of restorative justice, particularly in cases involving sexual abuse. Here's why it's essential and how it is promoted:

1. Understanding Harm: Encouraging participants, especially offenders, to understand the harm they've caused is crucial. This involves helping them grasp the emotional and psychological impact of their actions on survivors. It requires creating a safe space for survivors to express their feelings and needs, and for offenders to genuinely listen and comprehend the consequences of their behavior.

2. Empathy Building: Empathy involves putting oneself in another person's shoes and experiencing the situation from their perspective. Restorative justice processes use communication techniques, active listening, and non-violent communication to foster empathy among participants. Survivors' stories and experiences are shared in a way that helps offenders empathize with the pain and suffering they've caused.

3. Accountability: Encouraging accountability means holding offenders responsible for their actions. Offenders are encouraged to acknowledge the harm they've inflicted, express genuine remorse, and commit to making amends. This accountability is not punitive but aims to facilitate personal growth and responsibility-taking.

4. Apologies and Restitution: Restorative justice often includes opportunities for offenders to apologize directly to survivors and offer restitution when possible. These actions demonstrate accountability and a commitment to making things right.

5. Dialogue and Understanding: The restorative dialogue itself plays a significant role in encouraging empathy and accountability. When survivors and offenders engage in open and empathetic communication, they can better understand each other's perspectives, feelings, and needs.

6. Reconciliation: Ultimately, the goal is to foster reconciliation between survivors and offenders. This involves not only addressing the harm but also finding ways to move forward in a way that promotes healing and closure.

Empathy and accountability are intertwined in restorative justice. By encouraging offenders to understand the harm they've caused and by holding them accountable in a meaningful way, restorative justice seeks to promote healing and reconciliation for survivors while also facilitating the personal growth and rehabilitation of offenders. It aims to transform the dynamics of harm into an opportunity for understanding, repair, and, when possible, restoration of relationships.

CHAPTER 11

THE TRANSFORMATIVE POWER OF FORGIVENESS

The transformative power of forgiveness is a central theme within restorative justice, especially in cases of sexual abuse. It represents the potential for profound change and healing that forgiveness can bring. Here's an overview:

1. Healing and Closure: Forgiveness can be a source of healing for survivors. It allows them to release the emotional burden of anger, resentment, and pain associated with the abuse. Forgiving does not mean forgetting, but it can provide a sense of closure and liberation from the past.

2. Empowerment: Forgiveness can empower survivors by giving them agency over their emotions and decisions. It allows them to reclaim control over their lives and emotions, moving from victimhood to a position of strength.

3. Restoration of Relationships: In some cases, forgiveness can lead to the restoration of damaged relationships. When offenders genuinely take responsibility for their actions, express remorse, and make amends,

survivors may consider forgiveness as a step toward rebuilding trust.

4. Breaking the Cycle: Forgiveness can be a transformative force in breaking the cycle of harm. By addressing the root causes of abusive behavior and promoting accountability, forgiveness can contribute to the prevention of future abuse.

5. Emotional Freedom: Holding onto anger and resentment can be emotionally draining and harmful. Forgiveness can free survivors from these negative emotions, allowing them to focus on their well-being and future.

6. Accountability and Redemption: Forgiveness is not synonymous with absolution. Offenders must still be held accountable for their actions. Forgiveness can be an integral part of an offender's path toward redemption, as it involves taking responsibility and making amends.

Understanding forgiveness within the context of restorative justice is complex. It involves exploring what forgiveness means to survivors, whether they choose to forgive, and under what conditions. The transformative power of forgiveness lies in its potential to contribute to healing, reconciliation, and personal growth, both for survivors and, when appropriate, for offenders.

Challenges of Forgiveness:

Forgiveness can be a complex and challenging process, particularly in cases of sexual abuse. Some of the challenges survivors may face include:

1. Emotional Pain: Forgiveness often involves confronting painful emotions related to the abuse, such as anger, resentment, and grief. Facing these emotions can be difficult.

2. Fear of Invalidating Feelings: Survivors may fear that forgiving an offender might invalidate their own feelings and experiences or send a message that what happened was acceptable.

3. Lack of Genuine Remorse: Forgiveness may depend on whether the offender shows genuine remorse and takes meaningful steps toward amends. If the offender does not take responsibility or continues to deny the harm caused, forgiveness can be more challenging.

4. Pressure to Forgive: Survivors may feel pressured by society, family, or the restorative justice process to forgive, even when they are not ready or willing to do so.

Benefits of Forgiveness:

Despite the challenges, forgiveness can offer several potential benefits for both survivors and offenders:

1. Healing and Closure: Forgiveness can provide survivors with a sense of healing and closure, allowing them to move forward with their lives.

2. Empowerment: Forgiveness can empower survivors by giving them control over their emotions and decisions, allowing them to break free from the grip of anger and resentment.

3. Restoration of Relationships: In some cases, forgiveness can lead to the restoration of damaged relationships when offenders take responsibility and make amends.

4. Emotional Freedom: Forgiveness can free survivors from the emotional burden of holding onto anger and resentment, enabling them to focus on their well-being and future.

5. Accountability and Redemption: Forgiveness can be an integral part of an offender's path toward accountability and redemption, as it involves taking responsibility for one's actions and making amends.

6. Breaking the Cycle: Forgiveness can contribute to breaking the cycle of harm by addressing the root causes of abusive behavior and promoting accountability.

7. Community Healing: In cases involving the broader community, forgiveness can contribute to community healing and reconciliation, reducing the sense of division and conflict.

It's essential to recognize that forgiveness is a deeply personal and individual choice. While it can offer benefits, it should never be pressured or coerced. Survivors must decide for themselves whether forgiveness is a path they wish to pursue, and it should always be a voluntary and informed choice within the context of restorative justice processes.

Survivor Perspectives on Forgiveness:

In this section of the chapter, survivor perspectives on forgiveness are shared to provide real-world insights into this complex and deeply personal process. Survivors who have navigated the journey of forgiveness within the context of restorative justice offer their stories and insights:

1. Personal Healing: Some survivors share their experiences of forgiveness as a means of personal healing. They discuss how forgiving the offender allowed them to release the emotional pain and anger associated with the abuse, enabling them to find closure and move forward with their lives.

2. Empowerment: Survivors may express how forgiveness empowered them by giving them control over their emotions and decisions. They share how forgiving was a choice they made to free themselves from the emotional burden of holding onto anger and resentment.

3. Complex Emotions: Survivors acknowledge that forgiveness does not erase the pain or the harm they endured. They discuss the complex mix of emotions they experienced, including anger, sadness, and relief, while exploring the possibility of forgiveness.

4. Conditions for Forgiveness: Some survivors emphasize that their forgiveness was contingent on certain conditions, such as the offender taking genuine responsibility

for their actions, showing remorse, and actively participating in making amends.

5. Impact on Offenders: Survivors may share how their forgiveness impacted the offenders. They discuss whether forgiveness played a role in the offender's journey toward accountability and redemption.

6. Community and Restorative Justice: In cases involving the broader community, survivors reflect on how forgiveness contributed to community healing and reconciliation. They discuss the importance of restorative justice processes in facilitating these outcomes.

7. Challenges and Growth: Survivors may candidly discuss the challenges they faced on the path to forgiveness, including the fear of invalidating their own feelings or the difficulty of trusting the offender again. They also reflect on how forgiveness has contributed to their personal growth.

These survivor perspectives offer a diverse and nuanced understanding of forgiveness within the context of restorative justice. They illustrate that forgiveness is not a one-size-fits-all process but a deeply personal journey influenced by survivors' unique experiences, emotions, and conditions. By sharing their stories and insights, survivors contribute to a deeper appreciation of the complexities and transformative potential of forgiveness in the aftermath of sexual abuse.

CHAPTER 12

REINTEGRATION AND SUPPORT

Reintegration and support are essential components of the restorative justice process, particularly in cases of sexual abuse. Here's why they are important:

1. Continued Healing: Sexual abuse can have long-lasting effects on survivors and offenders alike. Reintegration and support are essential for facilitating continued healing and addressing the emotional and psychological aftermath of the abuse.

2. Accountability: Support systems play a role in holding offenders accountable for their commitments made during the restorative justice process. Monitoring and support help ensure that offenders fulfill their obligations, fostering a sense of accountability and responsibility.

3. Community Involvement: Reintegration and support involve the broader community, emphasizing that sexual abuse is not just an issue between survivors and offenders but a concern for the community as a whole. Community support can contribute to the healing and reconciliation process.

4. Prevention: By providing ongoing support and monitoring, reintegration efforts can help prevent reoffending by ensuring that offenders continue to address the root causes of their harmful behavior.

5. Empowerment: Support systems empower survivors by offering them a network of individuals and resources to lean on during difficult times. This empowerment aids in their ongoing recovery and personal growth.

6. Sustainability: Reintegration and support aim to create sustainable systems that can assist survivors and offenders in the long term. They recognize that the process of healing and accountability is not a one-time event but an ongoing journey.

7. Reducing Recidivism: By monitoring and supporting offenders in their commitment to making amends, reintegration efforts can contribute to reducing the likelihood of reoffending, enhancing community safety.

8. Community Healing: Reintegration and support contribute to community healing and reconciliation by involving community members in the restoration of relationships and trust.

In summary, reintegration and support are vital because they extend the restorative justice process beyond the initial dialogue and agreements. They provide ongoing assistance, accountability, and resources to survivors and offenders as they continue their journeys of healing, personal growth, and, when appropriate, reintegration into the community. These efforts reinforce the transformative potential of restorative justice in cases of sexual abuse.

Continued Healing:

Continued healing is a critical and lifelong journey for survivors of sexual abuse. Here's an overview of its significance and the strategies and resources associated with it:

Significance of Continued Healing:

1. Trauma Recovery: Survivors of sexual abuse often experience complex trauma that can persist for years. Continued healing is essential for addressing the ongoing effects of trauma and minimizing its impact on their lives.

2. Personal Growth: Healing is not just about recovering from trauma but also about personal growth and resilience. It allows survivors to build a stronger sense of self and move beyond the role of a victim.

3. Quality of Life: Continued healing contributes to an improved quality of life for survivors. It can lead to increased emotional well-being, better relationships, and a more fulfilling life.

4. Preventing Revictimization: Healing can empower survivors to recognize and avoid situations that may put them at risk of further victimization, reducing the likelihood of experiencing sexual abuse again.

Strategies and Resources for Continued Healing:

1. Therapy and Counseling: Many survivors benefit from therapy or counseling with trained professionals who specialize in trauma. These sessions provide a safe space to explore feelings, develop coping strategies, and work through the emotional aftermath of abuse.

2. Support Groups: Survivor support groups offer a sense of community and understanding. Sharing experiences and coping strategies with others who have faced similar challenges can be validating and healing.

3. Self-Care Practices: Self-care is crucial for continued healing. This includes activities such as meditation, mindfulness, exercise, and healthy eating, which promote emotional and physical well-being.

4. Education and Advocacy: Some survivors find empowerment in educating themselves about sexual abuse,

advocating for survivors' rights, and raising awareness about the issue.

5. Art and Creativity: Creative outlets, such as art, writing, or music, can be therapeutic and help survivors express their emotions and experiences.

6. Spiritual and Faith-Based Resources: For those who find solace in spirituality or faith, religious or spiritual practices can provide support and healing.

7. Safety Planning: Continued healing may involve developing safety plans to minimize the risk of further harm and to address triggers and potential challenges.

8. Professional Guidance: Consulting with professionals, such as trauma-informed therapists or counselors, can help survivors tailor a healing plan to their unique needs and circumstances.

Continued healing acknowledges that the journey toward recovery from sexual abuse is ongoing and that survivors may face different challenges at various stages of their lives. It emphasizes the importance of self-compassion, self-care, and accessing the resources and support needed to heal and thrive.

Accountability and Monitoring:

Accountability and monitoring are essential elements of the restorative justice process, especially in cases of sexual abuse. Here's an overview of their significance and how they are implemented:

Significance of Accountability:

1. Responsibility-Taking: Accountability requires offenders to take responsibility for their actions, acknowledging the harm they caused to survivors and the broader community.

2. Amends: Offenders are expected to make amends for the harm they caused. This may involve restitution,

community service, or other actions that contribute to the well-being of survivors and the community.

3. Prevention: Holding offenders accountable reduces the risk of reoffending. It encourages them to address the root causes of their harmful behavior and make changes to prevent future harm.

Mechanisms for Accountability and Monitoring:

1. Written Agreements: The restorative justice process often results in written agreements that outline the commitments made by both survivors and offenders. These agreements serve as a tangible record of the expectations and actions required.

2. Check-Ins: Periodic check-ins with offenders and survivors are essential for monitoring progress. Facilitators or restorative justice professionals can facilitate these meetings to ensure that commitments are being fulfilled.

3. Reports and Documentation: Offenders may be required to provide reports or documentation of their progress in fulfilling commitments. This documentation serves as evidence of accountability.

4. Community Involvement: The broader community may play a role in monitoring offenders' progress and providing support. Community members can act as accountability partners, helping offenders stay on track.

5. Mediation and Conflict Resolution: In cases where conflicts or challenges arise in fulfilling commitments, mediation and conflict resolution processes can be employed to address issues and find solutions.

6. Support Systems: Offenders may have support systems in place to assist them in fulfilling their commitments. This can include mentors, counselors, or community organizations.

7. Evaluation and Review: Periodic evaluations and reviews of the restorative justice process and outcomes ensure that the goals of accountability and monitoring are being met.

8. Sanctions for Non-Compliance: When offenders fail to fulfill their commitments or do not make genuine efforts to take responsibility, there may be consequences or sanctions, such as returning to the traditional criminal justice system.

Accountability and monitoring reinforce the principles of restorative justice by ensuring that the agreements reached during the restorative process are upheld. They provide survivors with assurance that offenders are taking meaningful steps to make amends for their actions. Additionally, they contribute to community safety by reducing the risk of reoffending and addressing the root causes of harmful behavior.

CHAPTER 13

CHALLENGES AND CRITICISMS

Restorative justice, particularly when applied to cases of sexual abuse, can face various challenges and criticisms. This section of the chapter addresses some of these concerns and explores strategies for addressing and mitigating them:

1. Safety Concerns: One of the primary concerns is the safety of survivors and the risk of retraumatization during the restorative justice process. Strategies for addressing this concern include ensuring safe environments, providing emotional support, and conducting thorough risk assessments.

2. Accountability: Critics may question whether restorative justice can sufficiently hold offenders accountable for their actions. Addressing this concern involves clear agreements, monitoring progress, and meaningful consequences for non-compliance.

3. Inequality of Power: Concerns about the power dynamics between survivors and offenders may arise. Restorative justice processes must be designed to address power imbalances and ensure that survivors have a voice and agency.

4. Consent: Obtaining informed and voluntary consent from survivors to participate in the restorative process is crucial. Critics may question whether survivors are pressured into participating. Ensuring that consent is freely given is a key element.

5. Reconciliation vs. Retribution: Critics may argue that restorative justice focuses too much on reconciliation at the expense of retribution or punishment. Addressing this concern involves emphasizing the importance of accountability and consequences for offenders.

6. Resource Limitations: Implementing restorative justice effectively requires resources, including trained facilitators and support services. Critics may raise concerns about resource limitations. Strategies for addressing this include training and capacity-building efforts.

7. Community Support: Restorative justice processes often involve the broader community, and concerns about community support may arise. Ensuring that communities are educated about restorative justice and its benefits can help address this concern.

8. Ethical Considerations: Ethical dilemmas related to confidentiality, impartiality, and fairness may be raised. Restorative justice practitioners must adhere to ethical principles and guidelines to navigate these concerns.

9. Reintegration of Offenders: Critics may question whether offenders can be successfully reintegrated into the community. Addressing this concern involves providing support and monitoring to ensure offenders are genuinely committed to change.

10. Measuring Success: Critics may challenge the ability to measure the success of restorative justice processes. Developing clear criteria and evaluation methods can help demonstrate their effectiveness.

Addressing these challenges and criticisms requires careful consideration, adaptation of restorative justice practices, and ongoing evaluation. Restorative justice practitioners and policymakers must be responsive to concerns and continuously strive to improve the process to ensure that it serves the best interests of survivors, offenders, and the broader community.

Ethical Considerations in Restorative Justice for Sexual Abuse:

Restorative justice, particularly in cases of sexual abuse, involves complex ethical considerations. Here are some of the key ethical dilemmas and principles that should guide practitioners:

1. Confidentiality: Practitioners must ensure the confidentiality of the restorative justice process while balancing the need for transparency and accountability. Maintaining the privacy and safety of survivors is paramount.

2. Impartiality: Restorative justice facilitators should remain impartial and not show favoritism toward either survivors or offenders. Fairness in the process is essential to maintain its integrity.

3. Informed Consent: Obtaining informed and voluntary consent from survivors to participate in the restorative process is an ethical imperative. Participants must fully understand the process, their rights, and their role.

4. Power Imbalances: Addressing power imbalances between survivors and offenders is crucial. Ethical practice involves ensuring that survivors have a voice, are treated with respect, and are not retraumatized by the process.

5. Survivor-Centered Approach: Ethical practitioners prioritize the needs and well-being of survivors. The process should be survivor-centered, focusing on their healing and empowerment.

6. Offender Accountability: Ethical restorative justice requires that offenders take genuine responsibility for their actions and make meaningful amends. Practitioners must ensure that accountability is not compromised.

7. Voluntary Participation: All participants, including offenders, should participate voluntarily. Coercion or pressure to participate is unethical.

8. Safety: Ensuring the physical and emotional safety of all participants is a fundamental ethical obligation. This includes risk assessment and crisis management plans.

9. Transparency: The process should be transparent and open, with clear communication about the goals, expectations, and outcomes. This transparency fosters trust among participants.

10. Cultural Sensitivity: Practitioners should be sensitive to cultural differences and ensure that the process respects and values diverse perspectives and traditions.

11. Continuous Improvement: Ethical practitioners are committed to continuous improvement. They engage in ongoing training, self-reflection, and adherence to ethical guidelines.

12. Evaluation and Accountability: Ethical considerations extend to the evaluation of the process. Practitioners should assess the impact of restorative justice and be accountable for its outcomes.

Navigating these ethical considerations requires practitioners to have a strong ethical framework, ongoing training, and a commitment to upholding the dignity and rights of all participants. Ethical practice ensures that the restorative justice process remains a tool for healing, accountability, and reconciliation in cases of sexual abuse.

Measuring Success in Restorative Justice for Sexual Abuse:

Measuring the success of restorative justice processes is vital to assess their impact and effectiveness, particularly in cases of sexual abuse. Here are key criteria and metrics used to evaluate the success of restorative justice in these contexts:

1. Survivor Satisfaction: The satisfaction and well-being of survivors are paramount. Success is measured by assessing whether survivors found the process supportive, empowering, and conducive to their healing. High levels of survivor satisfaction indicate a positive outcome.

2. Healing and Recovery: Success is measured by the extent to which survivors experience healing and recovery as a result of their participation in the restorative justice process. This includes reductions in trauma symptoms, improved mental and emotional well-being, and increased resilience.

3. Offender Accountability: Success involves holding offenders accountable for their actions. Metrics may include whether offenders fulfill their commitments, show genuine remorse, and take meaningful steps to make amends. Successful outcomes indicate that offenders are taking responsibility.

4. Prevention of Reoffending: Success can be measured by assessing whether offenders who have gone through the restorative justice process are less likely to reoffend. A reduction in recidivism rates is a positive indicator.

5. Community Healing: The success of restorative justice extends to the broader community. Metrics include whether the community experiences healing, reconciliation, and a restoration of trust. Successful outcomes reflect a positive impact on the community.

6. Victim-Offender Relationships: Successful restorative justice processes often result in improved relationships between survivors and offenders. Metrics may include whether survivors and offenders are able to

communicate constructively, achieve understanding, and, in some cases, reconcile.

7. Compliance with Agreements: Success is measured by the extent to which participants comply with the agreements reached during the restorative justice process. Compliance indicates a commitment to change and accountability.

8. Reduction in Retraumatization: The process should not retraumatize survivors. Success is assessed by whether survivors report reduced levels of emotional distress and trauma-related symptoms after participating.

9. Cost-Effectiveness: Evaluating the cost-effectiveness of restorative justice processes is essential. Success can be measured by comparing the resources required for restorative justice with the outcomes achieved, including reduced recidivism and improved well-being.

10. Ethical Adherence: Success includes adherence to ethical principles and guidelines throughout the process. Practitioners and participants must uphold ethical standards, ensuring that the process remains fair, respectful, and safe.

11. Participant Feedback: Gathering feedback from survivors, offenders, and other participants is valuable. Success is reflected in the feedback received, which can highlight areas of improvement and areas where the process is working effectively.

Measuring success in restorative justice for sexual abuse is a multifaceted endeavor that considers the well-being of survivors, accountability of offenders, community healing, and the ethical integrity of the process. These metrics help ensure that restorative justice processes are achieving their intended goals of healing, reconciliation, and accountability in cases of sexual abuse.

CHAPTER 14

GLOBAL PERSPECTIVE ON RESTORATIVE JUSTICE

Understanding the global perspectives on restorative justice in cases of sexual abuse is essential to appreciate the broad impact and diverse approaches taken in different regions. This chapter focuses on three key aspects:

1. International Initiatives: This section sheds light on the international efforts to promote restorative justice principles. It explores the work of organizations, governments, and advocates who strive to establish global standards and guidelines for implementing restorative justice in cases of sexual abuse. These initiatives aim to create a shared framework that transcends national boundaries and fosters collaboration among countries.

2. Cross-Cultural Approaches: Restorative justice is not a one-size-fits-all concept, and its application varies across cultures. This part of the chapter delves into how different cultural contexts interpret and implement restorative justice

principles when addressing sexual abuse cases. It underscores the importance of respecting cultural diversity and tailoring restorative justice practices to align with local norms and values.

3. Lessons from Different Jurisdictions: Learning from the experiences of various jurisdictions worldwide is invaluable. This section provides insights into the successes and challenges encountered when applying restorative justice to sexual abuse cases on a global scale. It highlights the exchange of best practices, the adaptability of restorative justice principles in different legal and cultural contexts, and the continuous improvement of restorative justice approaches through cross-jurisdictional learning.

By examining these global perspectives, the chapter aims to offer a comprehensive view of how restorative justice is evolving and being applied internationally in the context of sexual abuse. It emphasizes the collaborative efforts of individuals and entities working to make justice more healing and inclusive on a global scale.

Cross-Cultural Approaches to Restorative Justice: Restorative justice is not a one-size-fits-all concept, and its application varies across different cultural contexts worldwide. This section of the chapter delves into how various cultures interpret and implement restorative justice principles when addressing cases of sexual abuse. Here are some key aspects:

1. Cultural Interpretation: Different cultures have unique worldviews, values, and beliefs that influence their interpretation of justice and healing. Cross-cultural approaches explore how restorative justice aligns with or adapts to these cultural perspectives.

2. Cultural Sensitivity: Respecting cultural diversity is paramount in restorative justice. Practitioners must be sensitive to cultural nuances and avoid imposing Western-

centric models onto non-Western cultures. This approach ensures that justice processes are culturally appropriate and do not perpetuate harm.

3. Indigenous Practices: Many indigenous cultures have long-standing traditions of community-based conflict resolution and restoration. Cross-cultural approaches highlight the relevance and effectiveness of incorporating indigenous practices into restorative justice processes, especially in cases of sexual abuse.

4. Language and Communication: Communication styles and language play a significant role in cross-cultural restorative justice. Practitioners must consider language barriers, nuances in communication, and the importance of interpreters when facilitating dialogues involving participants from different cultural backgrounds.

5. Community Involvement: In some cultures, community involvement is integral to justice and healing. Cross-cultural approaches explore how community members can play active roles in the restorative justice process, offering support and reconciliation to survivors and offenders.

6. Balancing Tradition and Modernity: Cross-cultural approaches consider how restorative justice can strike a balance between preserving traditional cultural practices and integrating modern legal and human rights frameworks.

7. Learning from Indigenous Wisdom: Indigenous cultures often hold valuable wisdom regarding conflict resolution, restoration, and reconciliation. Cross-cultural approaches encourage the sharing of these insights to enhance restorative justice practices globally.

8. Challenges and Opportunities: This section discusses both the challenges and opportunities of applying restorative justice in diverse cultural contexts. It recognizes that cultural diversity enriches restorative justice but may also present complexities that require careful navigation.

Cross-cultural approaches to restorative justice underscore the importance of inclusivity, cultural sensitivity, and adaptability. They aim to ensure that restorative justice practices are not only effective but also respectful of the diverse cultural backgrounds of participants, fostering healing and justice within the context of sexual abuse cases.

Lessons from Different Jurisdictions in Applying Restorative Justice to Sexual Abuse Cases:

Learning from diverse jurisdictions provides valuable insights into the application of restorative justice to sexual abuse cases on a global scale. Here are some key lessons:

1. Cultural Adaptation: Different legal and cultural contexts require adaptation. Restorative justice principles can be effectively tailored to align with local norms and values while preserving the core principles of healing and accountability.

2. Legal Frameworks: The legal frameworks in various jurisdictions may impact the implementation of restorative justice. Successful cases often involve cooperation between legal systems and restorative justice practices.

3. Survivor-Centered Approaches: Jurisdictions that prioritize survivor well-being and empowerment within the restorative justice process tend to yield positive outcomes. Survivor-centered practices include providing support, ensuring safety, and offering choices.

4. Offender Accountability: Emphasizing offender accountability remains crucial. Jurisdictions that hold offenders responsible for their actions and monitor their compliance with agreements contribute to the effectiveness of restorative justice.

5. Community Involvement: Involving the community in the restorative process can enhance its impact. Communities provide support, reconciliation, and a sense of belonging for survivors and offenders.

6. Training and Education: Adequate training and education for practitioners are essential. Jurisdictions with well-trained facilitators and informed participants tend to have more successful outcomes.

7. Evaluation and Research: Continuous evaluation and research help refine restorative justice practices. Jurisdictions that invest in evaluating the effectiveness of their programs can make informed improvements.

8. Cross-Jurisdictional Learning: The exchange of best practices and lessons learned between jurisdictions is invaluable. Restorative justice practitioners and policymakers should collaborate and learn from one another's experiences.

9. Legal Recognition: Recognition and support from the legal system can bolster the effectiveness of restorative justice. Jurisdictions that integrate restorative justice into their legal systems provide survivors and offenders with more comprehensive support.

10. Flexibility: Restorative justice processes should be adaptable to various case-specific needs. Jurisdictions that allow flexibility in the process and outcomes tend to better address the complexities of sexual abuse cases.

11. Ethical Adherence: Upholding ethical principles, such as informed consent, confidentiality, and impartiality, is critical in all jurisdictions. Ethical practice ensures that the restorative justice process remains fair and respectful.

12. Collaboration: Collaboration among stakeholders, including government agencies, community organizations, and survivors' advocates, strengthens the impact of restorative justice. Jurisdictions that foster collaboration can provide a more comprehensive support system.

13. Survivor Voices: Amplifying the voices of survivors in shaping restorative justice practices is essential. Listening to survivor perspectives informs improvements and ensures that the process meets their needs.

These lessons underscore the dynamic and adaptable nature of restorative justice. They emphasize that while principles remain consistent, the application of restorative justice to sexual abuse cases may vary to accommodate the legal, cultural, and social contexts of different jurisdictions. By sharing experiences and learning from one another, global efforts to promote healing, accountability, and justice in cases of sexual abuse can continue to evolve and improve.

CHAPTER 15

ADVOCACY AND THE FUTURE OF RESTORATIVE JUSTICE

Advocacy for change and considering the future of restorative justice in sexual abuse cases are of paramount importance for several reasons:

1. Raising Awareness: Advocacy efforts play a crucial role in raising awareness about restorative justice as a viable and transformative approach for addressing sexual abuse. Increased awareness can lead to broader acceptance and adoption of these practices.

2. Policy Influence: Advocacy helps shape policies and legal frameworks. By advocating for restorative justice, organizations and activists can influence policymakers to integrate restorative principles into the justice system, leading to more supportive and survivor-centered policies.

3. Survivor Empowerment: Advocacy empowers survivors by giving them a platform to share their stories and advocate for their rights. It amplifies survivor voices and ensures their perspectives are considered in shaping the future of restorative justice.

4. Changing Societal Attitudes: Advocacy efforts work to change societal attitudes towards sexual abuse and justice. By challenging misconceptions and stigmas, advocates contribute to a more empathetic and understanding society.

5. Continual Improvement: Considering the future of restorative justice allows for ongoing innovation and improvement. By anticipating challenges and opportunities, practitioners and policymakers can adapt and refine restorative justice practices.

6. Transformative Potential: Restorative justice has the potential to transform the way society addresses sexual abuse, emphasizing healing, reconciliation, and accountability. Advocacy ensures that this potential is recognized and realized.

7. Survivor-Centered Approaches: The future of restorative justice should prioritize survivor-centered approaches. Advocacy helps maintain a focus on survivors' needs and ensures that restorative justice practices evolve to better serve them.

8. Addressing Systemic Issues: Advocacy can address systemic issues within the justice system, such as bias, discrimination, and disparities in access to justice. Restorative justice advocates work towards a more equitable and inclusive system.

9. Collaboration: Advocacy efforts foster collaboration among various stakeholders, including survivors, practitioners, policymakers, and community organizations. Collaboration is essential for effecting meaningful change.

10. Accountability: Advocacy holds institutions and systems accountable for addressing sexual abuse effectively. It monitors progress, highlights deficiencies, and demands accountability in the pursuit of justice.

In summary, advocacy and considering the future of restorative justice are essential components in the ongoing journey to create a more just and compassionate response to sexual abuse. They ensure that restorative justice continues to evolve, adapt, and be embraced as a powerful tool for healing, accountability, and reconciliation in cases of sexual abuse.

Policy Implications of Restorative Justice in Sexual Abuse Cases:

Understanding and addressing the policy implications of restorative justice in sexual abuse cases is crucial for several reasons:

1. Legal Framework: Policymakers play a pivotal role in establishing the legal framework for restorative justice practices in sexual abuse cases. They need to create legislation that recognizes and supports restorative justice processes, including issues related to informed consent, confidentiality, and legal recognition.

2. Funding and Resources: Adequate funding and resources are essential for the effective implementation of restorative justice programs. Policymakers must allocate resources to ensure that practitioners have the training, support, and infrastructure needed to conduct restorative processes safely and effectively.

3. Integration with the Criminal Justice System: Policymakers can facilitate the integration of restorative justice into the broader criminal justice system. This includes developing protocols for referrals to restorative processes, coordination between restorative justice practitioners and legal authorities, and ensuring that restorative justice complements rather than replaces traditional legal proceedings.

4. Survivor-Centered Policies: Policymakers should prioritize survivor-centered policies that prioritize survivors' needs and choices throughout the restorative justice process. This includes policies that provide access to support services,

protection from retraumatization, and opportunities for survivor participation in decision-making.

5. Ethical Guidelines: Developing and enforcing ethical guidelines for restorative justice practitioners is essential. Policymakers can establish standards of practice that ensure fairness, impartiality, informed consent, and confidentiality.

6. Public Awareness and Education: Policymakers can support public awareness campaigns and educational initiatives to inform the public about restorative justice and its potential benefits in cases of sexual abuse. This can help reduce stigmatization and misconceptions.

7. Evaluation and Research: Policymakers can fund and encourage research and evaluation of restorative justice programs in sexual abuse cases. This ensures that policies are based on evidence and that programs are continually improved.

8. Collaboration: Policymakers can facilitate collaboration among various stakeholders, including government agencies, community organizations, and survivors' advocates. Collaborative efforts help create a comprehensive and supportive system for restorative justice.

9. Equity and Inclusion: Policymakers should ensure that restorative justice practices are equitable and inclusive, addressing issues of access, cultural sensitivity, and the needs of marginalized communities.

10. Monitoring and Accountability: Policymakers must establish mechanisms for monitoring the effectiveness of restorative justice programs and holding practitioners accountable for ethical and professional conduct.

Addressing these policy implications is essential for creating an enabling environment where restorative justice can thrive as a valuable approach for addressing sexual abuse cases. Policymakers have the power to shape the legal and institutional frameworks that support survivors, promote accountability, and foster healing and reconciliation through restorative justice practices.

The future of restorative justice in sexual abuse cases holds both promise and challenges:

Advancements:

1. Increased Adoption: Restorative justice is likely to see increased adoption in sexual abuse cases as more jurisdictions recognize its potential for healing and accountability.

2. Technology Integration: Technology may play a role in expanding access to restorative processes, facilitating virtual dialogues, and ensuring confidentiality.

3. Research and Evaluation: Ongoing research and evaluation will refine restorative justice practices, leading to evidence-based improvements.

4. Cultural Integration: Restorative justice will continue to adapt to diverse cultural contexts, respecting local values while upholding its core principles.

5. Survivor Empowerment: The future will prioritize survivor empowerment, giving survivors more control over the process and outcomes.

Challenges:

1. Resistance: Resistance from traditional justice systems may persist, hindering the full integration of restorative justice.

2. Resource Allocation: Adequate funding and resources for restorative justice programs remain a challenge.

3. Stigmatization: Overcoming societal stigmatization and misconceptions about restorative justice in sexual abuse cases will require ongoing awareness campaigns.

4. Complex Cases: Restorative justice may face difficulties in addressing complex cases or those involving multiple survivors and offenders.

5. Cultural Sensitivity: Ensuring cultural sensitivity while maintaining ethical standards will continue to be a balancing act.

Opportunities:

1. Prevention: Restorative justice can play a role in prevention by addressing the root causes of sexual abuse and promoting education and awareness.

2. Community Healing: Communities can become more involved in the healing and restoration process, creating a network of support for survivors.

3. Global Collaboration: Cross-jurisdictional learning and collaboration can lead to the development of international standards and guidelines.

4. Legal Recognition: Increased legal recognition and integration into existing justice systems can enhance the effectiveness of restorative justice.

5. Rehabilitation: Restorative justice may contribute to the rehabilitation of offenders, reducing recidivism rates.

The future of restorative justice in sexual abuse cases depends on the commitment of practitioners, policymakers, survivors, and advocates to overcome challenges and seize opportunities. With a survivor-centered approach, ongoing research, ethical practice, and cross-cultural understanding, restorative justice has the potential to continue evolving as a transformative and healing response to the complex issue of sexual abuse.

CHAPTER 16

CONCLUSION: REFLECTING ON THE JOURNEY

As we conclude this journey through the book on restorative justice in sexual abuse cases, it's essential to reflect on the key concepts, principles, challenges, and successes that have been explored:

1. Understanding the Problem: Sexual abuse is a deeply troubling and pervasive issue that affects individuals and communities worldwide. It leaves profound physical, emotional, and psychological scars, challenging the very fabric of trust, safety, and justice in society.

2. The Need for a Restorative Approach: Traditional criminal justice systems often struggle to address the complexities of sexual abuse cases. The adversarial nature of trials, the focus on punitive measures, and the limited support available to survivors often leave them feeling unheard, unsupported, and retraumatized.

3. Core Concepts of Restorative Justice: Restorative justice principles, including accountability, empathy, and inclusivity, form the foundation of this transformative approach. These principles guide the restorative process and contribute to its effectiveness in cases of sexual abuse.

4. Historical Context and Evolution: Restorative justice has deep historical roots, including indigenous and traditional practices. It has evolved over time to adapt to changing societal needs and complexities.

5. Restorative vs. Retributive Justice: Contrasting restorative justice with retributive justice highlights the fundamental differences in their approaches. Restorative justice prioritizes healing, reconciliation, and the repair of harm, making it uniquely suited to address sexual abuse cases.

6. Prevalence and Impact of Sexual Abuse: The statistics and prevalence of sexual abuse underscore the urgent need to address this pervasive issue. The psychological and emotional impact on survivors is profound, and the societal implications extend to eroding trust, safety, and justice in communities.

7. Survivor Trauma: Survivors of sexual abuse carry deep trauma that affects their mental and emotional well-being. Understanding this trauma is essential for offering meaningful support and fostering healing.

8. Trauma-Informed Care: Trauma-informed care is a cornerstone in assisting survivors on their path to recovery. It emphasizes creating safe and supportive environments that acknowledge the impact of trauma.

9. Barriers to Disclosure: Survivors often face significant barriers when contemplating disclosure, including stigma, fear, and a lack of support. Recognizing and addressing these barriers is crucial.

10. Traditional Criminal Justice Responses: Traditional criminal trials have inherent limitations in addressing sexual abuse cases, including the burden of proof, retraumatization, and a focus on punishment over healing.

11. Role of Stakeholders: Various stakeholders, including facilitators, survivors, offenders, and communities, play critical roles in the restorative justice process. Building

trust and collaboration among these stakeholders is essential for success.

12. Preparing for a Restorative Process: Conducting initial assessments, obtaining informed consent, and implementing safety measures are crucial steps in preparing for a restorative justice process.

13. The Restorative Dialogue: Creating a safe space, using effective communication techniques, and encouraging empathy and accountability are essential elements of the restorative dialogue.

14. The Transformative Power of Forgiveness: Forgiveness, within the context of restorative justice, is complex. It presents challenges and benefits and is best understood through survivor perspectives.

15. Reintegration and Support: Developing support systems, fostering continued healing, and ensuring offender accountability and monitoring are integral aspects of the restorative justice process.

16. Challenges and Criticisms: Addressing concerns, ethical considerations, and measuring success are ongoing challenges in the application of restorative justice to sexual abuse cases.

7. Global Perspectives: Exploring international initiatives, cross-cultural approaches, and lessons from different jurisdictions provides valuable insights into the successes and challenges of applying restorative justice on a global scale.

18. Advocacy and the Future: Advocacy efforts, policy implications, and speculation on the future of restorative justice highlight the importance of promoting change, influencing policies, and envisioning a more just and compassionate response to sexual abuse.

This journey has taken us through a comprehensive exploration of restorative justice in the context of sexual abuse. It reminds us of the transformative potential of this approach to healing, accountability, and reconciliation. As we reflect on these concepts and principles, we are called to action—action that empowers survivors, advocates for change, and contributes to a more compassionate and just society for all.

Preface: Restorative Justice for Sexual Abuse

In the intricate tapestry of our societies, few issues are as deeply troubling and pervasive as sexual abuse. It is a dark cloud that looms over individuals and communities worldwide, leaving in its wake profound physical, emotional, and psychological scars. It challenges the very fabric of trust, safety, and justice upon which our societies are built. It is a topic that has long eluded easy solutions and clear answers.

This book, "Restorative Justice for Sexual Abuse," embarks on a transformative journey into the heart of this multifaceted issue. It recognizes the urgency of addressing sexual abuse in a way that not only holds offenders accountable but also fosters healing, reconciliation, and the restoration of shattered lives. It explores the possibilities and complexities of applying restorative justice principles to the most sensitive and intricate issues surrounding sexual abuse.

Our journey begins with a deep dive into the problem itself—understanding the intricacies of sexual abuse, recognizing it as a violation of one's autonomy and consent. We explore how it knows no boundaries of age, gender, race, or socioeconomic status, and how its consequences ripple through every corner of society. We learn the sobering realities of sexual abuse, examining its prevalence, impact, and the enduring trauma it inflicts upon survivors.

As we progress, we discover why there is a pressing need for a restorative approach. Traditional criminal justice systems often struggle to address the complexities of sexual abuse cases. The adversarial nature of trials, the focus on punitive measures, and the limited support available to survivors often leave them feeling unheard, unsupported, and retraumatized. It is here that we emphasize the importance of a restorative approach—an approach centered on healing, empathy, accountability, and the restoration of shattered lives. We explore how restorative justice principles can offer an alternative path to justice and recovery.

Delving further, we define the core principles of restorative justice, exploring concepts such as accountability, empathy, and inclusivity. We trace the historical roots and evolution of restorative justice, recognizing the rich tapestry of influences that have shaped this approach. We contrast restorative justice with retributive justice, highlighting why the former is uniquely suited to address the sensitive and intricate issues surrounding sexual abuse.

Our journey takes us through the prevalence and impact of sexual abuse, examining alarming statistics and the devastating psychological and emotional consequences it inflicts upon survivors. We also explore the broader societal implications of sexual abuse, recognizing that its repercussions extend far beyond individual survivors to erode trust in interpersonal relationships, undermine the sense of safety in communities, and challenge the effectiveness of justice systems.

Understanding survivor trauma is essential, and we delve deep into the intricate landscape of trauma experienced by survivors of sexual abuse. We also explore trauma-informed care—a cornerstone in the process of assisting survivors on their path to recovery—and the barriers that survivors often face when contemplating disclosure.

We then journey through the limitations of traditional criminal justice responses, understanding the challenges of criminal trials in addressing the complexities of sexual abuse cases. We examine the survivor's experience within the justice system, acknowledging the emotional and psychological toll it can take. We conclude by highlighting the issue of unresolved trauma within the traditional criminal justice system, setting the stage for our exploration of restorative justice as an alternative approach.

The heart of this book lies in the introduction to restorative justice for sexual abuse. We introduce core concepts and principles that underpin this transformative approach. We provide case studies of successful restorative approaches, illustrating their effectiveness in addressing the needs of survivors, holding offenders accountable, and promoting healing and reconciliation.

We explore the critical roles played by various stakeholders in the restorative justice process, including facilitators, survivors, offenders, and communities. We emphasize the importance of building trust and collaboration among these stakeholders, recognizing that the success of restorative justice hinges on their collective efforts.

Preparing for a restorative process is essential, and we delve into initial assessments, informed consent, and safety measures. We establish the groundwork for the restorative dialogue—an essential component of the process. Creating a safe space, utilizing communication techniques, and encouraging empathy and accountability are explored in-depth.

Forgiveness is central to restorative justice, and we delve into its complexities, challenges, and benefits. We provide survivor perspectives on forgiveness, offering real-world insights into this intricate concept.

Our journey continues with a focus on reintegration and support, understanding the importance of developing support systems, fostering continued healing, and ensuring accountability and monitoring of offenders.

We address the challenges and criticisms that may arise in the application of restorative justice, examining concerns, ethical considerations, and measures of success. We explore global perspectives on restorative justice, including international initiatives, cross-cultural approaches, and lessons from different jurisdictions.

The conclusion reflects on the journey we have taken—a journey that has delved deep into the complexities of sexual abuse and the transformative potential of restorative justice. It offers hope for healing and transformation and issues a call to action for readers to consider their roles in advancing the cause of restorative justice for sexual abuse.

This book is not just a collection of words; it is a journey of understanding, empathy, and hope. It is an invitation to explore an alternative approach to addressing one of the most challenging issues of our time. It is a testament to the resilience of survivors, the dedication of advocates, and the potential for healing and reconciliation. We hope that this journey will inspire change, ignite compassion, and contribute to a world where justice is not only blind but also healing and restorative.